A Short History of Beijing

JONATHAN CLEMENTS is a historian specialising in East Asia. His books include *A Brief History of China*, *The Art of War: A New Translation*, *The Emperor's Feast: A History of China in Twelve Meals* and biographies of Chairman Mao, Marco Polo, Khubilai Khan and the statesman and explorer Gustaf Mannerheim. His biographies of Empress Wu and the First Emperor of China and his history of the Silk Road have been translated into Chinese. He has appeared as an expert on Asian history in episodes of the TV programmes *Secret History* and *Nova*. For the National Geographic channel, he has presented several seasons of *Route Awakening*, a TV series on the historical origins of Chinese cultural icons, as well as the documentary *Shandong: Land of Confucius*.

PRAISE FOR THE FIRST EDITION, *AN ARMCHAIR TRAVELLER'S HISTORY OF BEIJING*

'This book is like having a friendly, knowledgeable companion taking your arm as you wander through the back alleys and boulevards of one of the world's great cities. Clements wears his learning lightly, and his informed but inclusive tone makes this the perfect book for the visitor to Beijing.' — Rana Mitter, author of *Modern China: A Very Short Introduction*

'Beijingers, both Chinese and foreign, mourn the Chinese capital's rapidly disappearing traditional alleys, but few of us appreciate Beijing as a city that has lasted through 2,500 years of building and destruction. Jonathan Clements' tour of the city starts with Peking Man and a jovial candy seller, and moves on through the Chinese dynasties with a readable flair. He comes well-stocked with tales that will be new even to long-time residents. It's a book for a warm teahouse on a cold winter afternoon.' — Lucy Hornby, Former China correspondent, *Financial Times*

'It's hard to imagine anyone better equipped than Clements to compile a readable account of Beijing. Authoritative yet deliciously irreverent, his history of the city is an essential companion for the visitor and a treasure trove of vicarious delights for the chair-bound.' — John Keay, author of *China: A History*

A Short History
of Beijing

Jonathan Clements

First published in Great Britain in 2016 as
An Armchair Traveller's History of Beijing by
The Armchair Traveller
4 Cinnamon Row, London SW11 3TW

This first paperback edition published in 2022 by Haus Publishing Ltd

Some parts of this book also previously appeared in *Beijing: Biography of a City* (Sutton Publishing, 2008)

Map on p. ix created by Martin Stiff

A CIP catalogue record for this book is available from the British Library

ISBN: 978-1-913368-46-3
eISBN: 978-1-913368-47-0

Typeset in Garamond by MacGuru Ltd

Printed in the United Kingdom by Clays Ltd (Elcograf S.p.A.)

For Julie Makinen

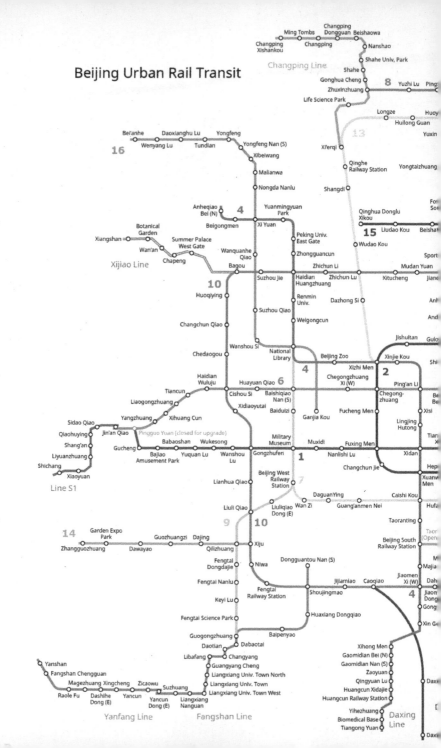

Contents

Acknowledgements

Parts of this book previously appeared in a substantially different form as *Beijing: The Biography of a City* (Sutton Publishing, 2008). Neither subject nor author was the same eight years later, when this book appeared in hardback, or six years after that for this paperback edition. The volume you are reading draws on much new development in China's capital, particularly the growth of its subway from a mere two lines on my first visit to today's twenty-four, and the new ease this affords the tourist for getting around. Professor Li Qi, of Xi'an Jiaotong University, made my visits to China much easier by appointing me a visiting professor from 2013 to 2019. For Beijing itself, advice and hints were at hand from Alicia Noel, Chris and Randa Westland, Wang Xue'er and Qiao Zhilin, who so sweetly trawled second-hand bookshops in search of a copy of the *Lao Beijing Lüxing Zhinan*. I also gratefully acknowledge the work of 'Ran' and 'Hat600' for their efforts not only in compiling an up-to-date English-language subway map but in making it available under a creative commons licence.

Julie Makinen and her sometime flatmate Lillian Chou were welcoming hosts in the diplomatic quarter, introducing me to the joys of Little Moscow, the Central Business District and the hippest of hipster hutongs. Louisa Lim and Amy Li Xuebai invited me to their restaurants, Southern Barbarian (Yunnan food, now sadly gone) and

Pak Pak (Thai food, still clinging on after COVID-19), and discussed the intricacies of running a business in Beijing – skulduggery, bribes, double-crosses and all. On many occasions, I have been accompanied by friends, relatives and colleagues, whose whims and caprices have often dragged me to places I would not have otherwise been: Emily Carlson; Kati Clements; Andrew Deacon; Philipp and Sara Holtkamp; Raija, Matias, Timo and Seija Mäki-Kuutti; Henri Pirkkalainen; and Tino Warinowski. My son Alexander spent much of his early life in China and was never a burden on explorations of the city together, leading me into many new and unexpected encounters, including the time he was savaged by a rabbit at the zoo and the time he decided to rush the security fence at Mao's mausoleum.

Introduction

Wangfujing, the best-known shopping street in Beijing, is wide and pedestrianised, dotted with interactive sculptures of merchants, artisans and musicians. It is the only street in the world where a visitor can get their watch fixed (at the Hengdeli watchmakers), dine on Beijing duck and/or a scorpion kebab, shop for nappies in the Children's Store, and bungee-jump from the roof of the Lisheng sports store.

Despite its sanitised, modern appearance, and its thick cluster of shopping malls, Wangfujing is steeped in history. The street boasts two museums, unnoticed by the casual stroller: an archaeological exhibition of Palaeolithic hunters, hidden inside the Oriental Plaza mall, and the Beijing Arts and Crafts Museum, tucked away on the fourth floor of an unassuming shop.

Somewhere near the Apple Store, Stone Age hunters once tracked deer through a lost forest. Just over the road from the Donglaishun hotpot restaurant, a Manchu prince made his fortune by sinking one of the city's few reliable wells.

St Joseph's Catholic Cathedral is actually the fourth church on that site. Where skateboarders now mill and leap in its courtyard, 'Boxer' rebels once charged the building with firebrands and swords, intent on murdering the Christians who had sought sanctuary within.

Look more closely at some of the less impressive stores to see evidence of their places in the history of shopping. The Silian Hair Salon, for example, comes spattered with gold plaques recording its important heritage; it might be just a hairdresser's to you, but throughout the 1970s this was the only place in Beijing where it was possible to get a perm – and, even then, only if clients supplied documentation proving it was necessary for their work. Just as deceptively unremarkable, the China Photo Studio was once based in Shanghai but was relocated to Beijing by government decree in 1956, whereupon it became the purveyor of photography to government officials.

Wangfujing has not always been known by this name. For a period of the twentieth century, it was called Morrison Street, named for George Morrison, the Australian journalist who became an adviser to several Chinese presidents. Morrison's house once stood here, although its location was bulldozed long ago to make way for the Beijing Department Store. This, too, was once a site of historical importance, the first such shopping experience in the Communist capital.

There is a statue outside, but it depicts someone quite unlikely. Chairman Mao is not celebrated here, nor is Premier Zhou Enlai, who waited meekly in line among bus drivers and shop girls to have his portrait taken at the China Photo Studio across the street. There is not even a statue to George Morrison, despite all he did for China; the street lost his name in 1949.

Passers-by might assume that the bronze bust of the laughing man, broad-shouldered in a suit, is some sort of politician or perhaps a vainglorious entrepreneur sticking his own effigy outside his main branch. But it is none of these things. The statue outside the Beijing Department Store is Zhang Binggui, the man who used to run the candy counter.

In 1950s Beijing, if there were sweets to be had, Zhang was the man who sold them. He always had a ready smile for his customers and the savant-like skill to weigh a handful of candy without recourse to scales. This stood him in good stead when a big shipment arrived – on the shop's busiest-ever day, he sold two tonnes of candy in just three hours to a scrum of eager customers.

An understandable hit with the kids, Zhang Binggui was proclaimed to be a model worker of the People's Republic. He became the subject of children's books about hard work and good manners. His picture appeared in national periodicals. He died in 1987, and his son still runs the counter in his father's jovial style. You can go there today and buy half a kilo of gobstoppers.

There is something about the statue of Zhang Binggui that encapsulates the charm of Beijing for me. Cynics may scoff at the grandstanding and consumerism; doubters may smirk at the sop thrown to the little people, in a country that still boasts mountainous images of dictators and war-lords. But there is something touching about the choice in priorities, and in the assertion, often repeated in Communist iconography, that the people are the heroes now. Zhang sold liquorice laces and humbugs for a living, and they built a statue to him because he made the children smile.

The Ming- and Qing-era historical city of Beijing is

entirely contained within the five-kilometre radius of the Second Ring Road, which follows the route of the old city walls. However, Beijing municipality covers 16,000 square kilometres and has an official population of 21.8 million – it is likely soon to out-people the whole of Australia. Its earliest archaeological relics of human habitation are half a million years old. In other words, it is no ordinary city, and any concise account such as this one faces an impossible task. I have chosen to focus on several key transformations in Beijing's history, in order to give the armchair traveller and real-world visitor a firm grounding in the way the city came to be. In the chapters that follow, you will read of the city's forgotten past as a kingdom in its own right, its centuries as little more than ruins and its restoration as the capital of a khan, the seat of Emperors and the prize of war-lords. The closing chapters deal with the city's recent past as the headquarters of Chinese Communism and its meteoric modernisation in the last thirty years.

The British traveller Mrs Alec Tweedie wrote in 1926:

One of the lures of Peking is old temples, old gates, massive walls of ancient days, and another is the street life. That life is always new, varied and wonderful. Every day one sees something one has never seen before, and every day one enjoys it more. It is all so unique, so unlike anywhere or anything else. Its passing is sad. Poor, dear, dirty, tumble-down, peeling Peking.

There are many guides to Beijing, and all tell the same story. Chinese tradition rarely recognises an inherent value in a mere building – houses and palaces are often nothing but bricks, beams and tiles, liable to burn or fall down, and easily replaced. It is a location itself, its natural features and history, which endures. In their book *In Search of Old Peking* (1935), L.C. Arlington and William Lewisohn lamented the difficulties of writing an accurate guidebook to Beijing and the possibility that readers might become irritated when they were unable to find monuments or buildings about which they had read:

> This, unfortunately, is not the fault of the authors – they would be only too glad if it was – but is due to the indifference of the Chinese themselves, more especially of their authorities, towards the historical monuments in which Peking is so rich. The loss by vandalism and utter neglect has been proceeding at such a rate that, on repeated occasions, buildings and historical monuments have actually disappeared while the authors are still writing about them.

Their complaint is a common one, repeated throughout history. Singers of the Dark Ages lamented the overgrown ruins of what had been the capital of the Land of Swallows. Retreating Mongols bemoaned the fate of their once-great 'khan's city', doomed – or so they thought – to fall into disrepair. In 2006, as I walked the dingy, grey paths of a 1950s slum, my companion announced sorrowfully that this, too, would soon pass, demolished to make way for Olympic hotels. Perhaps, hundreds of thousands of years ago, Peking Man looked over the rubble of his fallen cave roof, shook his head and grunted that the place was falling apart.

When Arlington and Lewisohn wrote, they were scathing about the removal of priceless treasures to the south. What would they have said if they had known what we know now, that those same treasures were not 'doomed to be eaten by moths, or destroyed by the damp'? Instead, they were spirited away to Taiwan, where they remain, regarded by some as an act of outrageous theft and by others as an act of fortuitous mercy. Had the retreating Republicans not taken the treasures with them, they might have been destroyed forever during the chaos of Mao's Cultural Revolution.

The early Communist era saw much of the old city demolished to make way for modernisation. Palaces were turned into dormitories; the city walls were pulled down to make space for a ring road. Tiananmen Square, that internationally infamous void at China's heart, is a relatively recent part of the city's mythos – it is the product of town-planning one-upmanship during the Cold War, when Mao was determined to have a parade ground to rival Moscow's Red Square. The twenty-first century has seen even more invasive demolition, as entire communities of old-fashioned housing are bulldozed to make way for yet more shopping malls. As little as 4% of Beijing's traditional buildings survive in 2022, and the bulk of those are concentrated in the Forbidden City.

Over the last few years, I have experienced a frustration that Arlington and Lewisohn would have found all too familiar. I have written up notes on a street of artisans or a wonderful restaurant, only to return a year later and find them replaced by a Louis Vuitton outlet or a kung-fu-themed noodle franchise. But this is a biography of a living, changing subject. This book will tell you Beijing's story – how the city has looked to thousands of generations of its inhabitants; its legends; and its tales of rags to riches, to rags again and riches once more.

Despite its modern incarnation as the quintessence of China, Beijing sits at the crossroads of cultures. For many centuries of its history, it has not been a wholly 'Chinese' city at all, since some of its most influential denizens have been from cultures that Chinese histories disparagingly dismissed as 'barbarian'. It is only in the last century that we have seen a change in perspective that now regards all ethnicities in China as 'Chinese'. The likes of the Manchus and Mongols are no longer regarded as foreign philistines (as they are described in the annals of their enemies), but as subsets of a great melting pot of fifty-six races, of which the 'Han' majority represent a 90% share.

Many such 'barbarians' were assimilated; some, like the Mongols and the Manchus, are indistinguishable to the average Westerner from the Chinese themselves. Such reversals of fortune have led to multiple name changes over the years – Beijing has been the South Capital, Tranquil City, Northern Peace, the Middle City, the Great Metropolis, the Place of Thistles and the Bitter Sea. In an effort to keep things simple, I refer to it throughout this book as Beijing, 'North Capital', even though it did not really gain that distinction until 1403.

Dynasties

Many guides translated for foreign visitors still assume that the tourist knows their Ming from their Qing. It is hence worth acquainting oneself with the broad spread of the Chinese dynasties, not so much for understanding this book as for appreciating some of the asides and short-hands of the average tour guide or museum signage.

These are the ones that are relevant for a visitor to Beijing:

Ancient China

Zhou Dynasty (time of Confucius)	1100–221 BC
Qin Dynasty (time of the First Emperor)	221–207 BC
Han Dynasty (China as a huge empire)	206 BC–AD 220

Early Medieval China

Sui Dynasty (China reunited)	581–618
Tang Dynasty (height of the Silk Road)	618–907
Song (North and South)	960–1279
Liao (north including Beijing ruled by Khitans)	916–1125
Jin (north including Beijing ruled by Jurchens)	1115–1234

Late Medieval China

Yuan (conquest by the Mongols; Beijing falls in 1215)	1271–1368
Ming (capital moves to Beijing in 1403)	1368–1644

The Modern Period

Qing (Manchu conquest, Empress Dowager,
  Last Emp.)   1644–1912
Republic (Yuan Shikai, Sun Yatsen,
  Japanese invasion)*   1912–1949
People's Republic (Chairman Mao
  et al.)   1949–present day

---

* The Republic of China continues on Taiwan to this day.

The Land of Swallows:
Prehistory to 221 BC

He is barely human. The nose is a little broader than one might be used to. The lips seem oddly thin, pressed in the beginnings of a smirk. Bushy eyebrows sit atop large brow ridges. He stares down the steps, towards what is now the car park, and seems lost in thought.

This is no ordinary sculpture. The bronze head that sits outside the Zhoukoudian museum is based on painstaking archaeological reconstruction. The artist Lucile Swan, a graduate of the Art Institute of Chicago, had moved to China in 1929, and found herself charged with the job of rebuilding the image of a man from mere fragments of bone. It was not the only sculpture that Swan worked on in Beijing. She also modelled a bust of Pierre Teilhard de Chardin, a Jesuit priest with whom she fell in love. They never consummated their relationship, although their passionate, heartfelt correspondence survives, as does Swan's statue of the famous 'Peking Man'. Today he stares, inscrutably, down the steps that lead up to the museum built in his honour.

The Discovery of Peking Man

Only a hundred years ago, Zhoukoudian was still an obscure mining community on the outskirts of Beijing, where residents quarried the nearby limestone hills. One cliff, known as Chicken Bone Hill, was notorious for its endless supply of old animal remains. Its artefacts were not always readily recognised – it also contained many fossils of unidentified creatures, written off by local authorities as 'dragon bones'.

Still beyond the reach of the modern subway network, Zhoukoudian doesn't attract the same dutifully trudging crowds as the Forbidden City. There are no truant students here trying to press-gang me into looking at their art show. No old ladies push postcards or souvenir fans. Zhoukoudian is a way out from the urban centre and chiefly of interest to archaeologists. On the day that I arrive, the car park is deserted. I have the gift shop to myself; the road to the summit is deserted and, at its terminus, I am the only man in the cave where the first men once dwelt.

A few foreign archaeologists picked over the area in the early twentieth century and carted off some debris to analyse. It was not until 1926, in Sweden, that scientists picking over some Zhoukoudian junk made the discovery of a lifetime – two human teeth. The first documented case of *Homo erectus pekinensis*, or Peking Man, had already travelled thousands of miles from the place where he, his ancestors and his distant descendants had made their homes for tens of thousands of years.

A wide, clean road leads up the hill to the museum, flanked by memorial tablets to the scholars who excavated Peking Man and his artefacts – men such as Johan Gunnar

Andersson, the Swedish geologist who surveyed the hill in 1918; Pei Wenzhong, the Chinese archaeologist who found the first skull in 1929; and Pierre Teilhard de Chardin, the French palaeontologist who was denounced by the Catholic church as a heretic.

A path winds away from the low, unobtrusive museum around the hilltop itself, where cavemen spent thousands of years looking down on the valley below. A single glance is not enough to appreciate its full impact. It is not the cave that is impressive, but the fact that primitive man lived here for thousands of years. This bare cavern could be the very place where fire was first kindled, where the first words were spoken, where the first art was created in China. Like the Great Wall, it is not so much the sight itself that is humbling; it is the knowledge of how far it extends beyond view, out past the horizon, across the mountains and deep back into time.

Time, not mere hours and days, but *geological* time, has changed this environment. A once-great river, where Peking Man fished and paddled, has shifted hundreds of miles to the south. Many of the caves have been carefully torn apart in the interests of science, and are only now being restored to their previous state. But *which* previous state? Here there was once a soaring, vaulted hall of shadows, the limestone walls sweating with spring water, a place used by generations of animals in search of a safe den. Millennia later, it was a split-level caveman apartment, its lower reaches used for burials and refuse.

Standing at the lowest point of the Zhoukoudian excavations, you gaze upward at a towering rock face, layers marked with occasional numbers. What was once a great cavernous fissure, as high as a football pitch is long, has slowly filled up over the centuries. At its lowest level, there is nothing save scattered lumps of ancient hyena faeces, scuffed and ground into the rock. But after thousands of years of occasional hyena habitation, the cave gains a new coating of red silt, as if new rains have washed mud from a new river somewhere nearby. Amidst the sandy clay are pieces of human fossil, animal bones and pieces of stone worked into scrapers and primitive axes.

Five hundred thousand years ago, Peking Man had arrived. The area was a lush, secluded valley, rich in game and plants. Peking Man hid from leopards, sabre-toothed tigers and bears, in an environment that was a home to porcupines, woolly rhinoceros and gazelles. He hunted these animals, luring the larger ones into a cave with a sudden vertical drop where he could finish them off at his leisure, cooking their meat on the first fires, scraping their skins to make the first rudimentary clothes. 'Suddenly', if anything can be sudden in geological time, Peking Man lost his furry covering and became a naked ape in need of animal skins to keep out the cold. He had become Upper Cave Man – *Homo sapiens*. Us.

Some have been harsh about Peking Man's culture. He has been accused of being a scavenger, not a hunter. His rudimentary stone 'chopping' tools have been unfavourably compared with the 'axes' of his European cousins, although recent research has suggested that the easy availability of bamboo in China probably led to much more sophisticated tools that rotted away many centuries ago.

It has been suggested that he did not master fire quite as early as some believed. Of the human remains at Zhoukoudian, 40% are those of children under fourteen years of age. Only 2.6% made it to fifty. His living arrangements have been ridiculed by modern observers who note not the fact of his survival, but the seemingly endless centuries in which so little changed, and early man huddled in the draughty, smoky gloom, chewing on the dirty, half-burnt, half-raw carcasses of bats.

One day, the sky fell in. The roof collapsed, leaving half the former cave open to the elements. The tribe of Peking Man relocated to the caves which still offered some protection from the outside world. They lived there for another eleven thousand years.

The Waste of the Bitter Sea
There is something truly daunting about the history of Beijing – a place inhabited by humankind since before they were human, for literally hundreds of thousands of years. Ruins on the landscape mark the places where ancient reasons for habitation have disappeared; place names recall the locations of dead springs, dried-up lakes and forgotten boundaries. There are hills in the Beijing area created by human hands using soil and rocks dragged up to make great lakes. Beijing is also the place where subhuman savages fought with bears and hyenas for shelter in mountain caves, where some of the first men hid from beasts now extinct.

When the distant successors of Peking Man were able to talk, they told stories about their forebears. The Chinese sage Confucius, among others, recognised that the ancestors of the Chinese had lived like beasts, cowering in the dark from the winter cold, and sleeping in trees during the summer heat:

> Formerly the ancient kings had no houses. In winter they lived in caves which they had excavated, and in summer in nests, which they had framed. They knew not yet the transforming power of fire, but ate the fruits of plants and trees, and the flesh of birds and beasts, drinking their blood and swallowing [also] the hair and feathers. They knew not yet the use of flax and silk, but clothed themselves with feathers and skins. (*Book of Rites* VII:1:viii)

The traditional centre of Chinese civilisation was far to the south in Luoyang, far along the Yellow River valley. But the Beijing region retained an important role in early Chinese folklore. It was, after all, inhabited for a long time. Thirty thousand years before the present day, Beijing was the place where Ice Age glaciers reached their southernmost moraine. It was the edge of the known world, looking southward to the plains of agrarian civilisation and north into the mountains, steppes and forests of the wilderness. According to legend, it was where man first tried to tame the elements, particularly fire and water.

There is a precarious cast to life on China's central lands. The Yellow River's floodplain stretches for hundreds of miles, creating a volatile environment in which the river can all too easily change course. Some of the 'smaller' rivers in north China have at times been part of the main course of the Yellow River, while some canals were actually dredged along the beds of forgotten, dried-up tributaries. Nor is water management a catch-all solution – the vast quantities of silt that give the river its name are easily dumped on its bed and banks, allowing it to swell over dams and break through levees, to the great danger of communities along its length. The result created a fear and respect for the mighty river throughout the time of Chinese legends.

The Beijing plain was almost uninhabitable for many centuries. Once the glacier snowmelt ran out, the rivers' continued retreat turned the lowlands into a brackish marsh stretching for many miles towards the sea, where reeds rocked in the wind across a long expanse of treacherous boggy ground. This, say the ancient legends, was the Waste of the Bitter Sea, home of a family of hateful dragons, who poisoned the surrounding area in an attempt to hold humans at bay. These dragons pop up on several occasions in Beijing's history, taking the blame for local natural disasters and reversals of fortune. Long into recorded history, Beijing's struggle for fresh water frequently elicited comments about the dragons in its midst, who had to be opposed, appeased, avoided.

Chinese mythology is a garbled mass of stories about ancient conflicts between godlike beings and earthbound tribes. Amid the slow expansion of numerous animal-totem tribes, two warring factions eventually called a truce. A man called the Yellow Sovereign, regarded by posterity as the ancestor of all the Chinese, led a confederation of totems, largely named after types of bear and big cat. They joined forces with another group, the Shennong people, possibly an alliance of nomad herders with pastoral farmers. This new confederation ran into another tribe somewhere in north-east China, where they fought over the precious resources of the plain of the Yellow River.

Accounts differ as to the identity of the rival leader. Some call him Shennong, using the name of the tribe with which the Yellow Sovereign's people had already merged. Others name him Chi You and call him a son of Shennong. Whoever this individual was, he is said to have led over seventy different tribes into battle.

Ancient Chinese texts describe Chi You as a veritable demon, with horns on his head and fleshy bat-wings that allowed him to fly, leading an army of giants, Koreans and evil spirits. His eighty-one brothers supposedly had the power of human speech but the bodies of beasts. To hear them described, they sound more like tanks, with bronze skulls, iron foreheads and a diet of rocks and stones. He had the power to transform his appearance and magical powers that permitted him to command the wind and rain in his service. Legend recounts that they met in a single colossal battle, although the events described go on for literally weeks and months.

The Yellow Sovereign charged onto a battlefield obscured by a magical mist and was forced to fall back on sorceries of his own. He used a magnetic device to determine directions (said to be the world's first compass) and employed the services of his daughter, Drought Fury, to somehow desiccate the air. Even then, the battle was not over. Chi You himself was hunted down by the dragon Yinglong, who killed him, and was cursed to remain forever on Earth in punishment.

The scattered remnants of Chi You's people fled far to the south-west, where, many generations later, after many further migrations, they evolved into the peripheral tribes known in Vietnam as the Hmong. To this day, Chi You is worshipped by the Hmong as a war god, and their term for him, pronounced in their own dialect as *Txiv Yawg*, means grandfather-ruler.

All this supposedly happened around 2500 BC, on the plains close to where Beijing now stands. As the capital of the Yellow Sovereign, this legendary (and archaeologically unknown) Beijing was a symbol of the order that the Yellow Sovereign brought to Earth, walls against the elements and channels dug to carry water.

The story of the Yellow Sovereign is rich in water symbolism – spirits of rain, drought and flood warring for control of a world – the mighty torrents of the river rebelling against the farmers who thought they had tamed them. Not for nothing is the unpredictable Yellow River sometimes known as China's Sorrow, in memory of the millions killed by its sudden shifts in direction. But with the Yellow River turning southward, away from its former course, the region became less important.

Even if this legendary Beijing were a real place, it was soon marginalised in the eyes of the Chinese. The descendants of the legendary Yellow Sovereign moved ever westwards, eventually settling far upstream. Although the region where Beijing now stands was regarded as part of China by the earliest Chinese, it was still on the edge of the known world. As the legendary divinities of antiquity began their slow segue into a list of historical kings, north-east China became one of a handful of dukedoms that paid fealty to the rulers of the Zhou dynasty.

The Place of Thistles

There is another forgotten conflict, unrecorded in the Chinese histories, but apparent from place names. Where solid ground met marshland and lakes, facing the plains of reeds stretching towards the sea, there was a village called Ji, 'the Thistles'. Its inhabitants were eventually absorbed into another group, the Yan – a picturesque name meaning 'the Swallows'.

The Place of Thistles became a community within the Land of Swallows, named for the flocks of darting birds that can still be seen in its skies. Ji remained a town within the Yan domains, but a few centuries later the conqueror's capital was abandoned in favour of Ji itself. Perhaps it was indefensible from northern barbarians; perhaps another well dried up, or floodwaters rose. Whatever the reason, Ji enjoyed a new lease of life – for the first time, the place we now call Beijing was the capital of a country.

The people of the Swallows made their homes in and among the people of the Place of Thistles. Ji became Yanjing, Capital of the Swallows, a poetic name that can still be found sometimes on products and services in the Beijing area.

The 'city', identified from a handful of bronze artefacts unearthed in the south-west of modern Beijing, was a small enclosure, barely 850 metres across, encircled by an earth rampart. Archaeology has determined that the site itself was larger, perhaps two miles across, implying that the original fort soon attracted settlers who built their homes outside its walls.

The Land of Swallows was originally founded as a border march – a place where a military garrison might watch the mountains for signs of invaders from the north. The Great Wall of China began life in the north of the Land of Swallows, although in a far less majestic incarnation than the one known today. Despite such potential dangers north of its borders, there were many periods in the history of the region where the supposed 'barbarians' were friendly, contained, absent or simply otherwise occupied. During such years, the state of Yan was widely regarded as a paradise, insulated by its outlying location from much of the diplomatic pushing and shoving of other early Chinese states. It was also blessed with good natural resources. Even the mountains on its northern border could be refashioned as south-facing agricultural slopes.

Su Qin, a famous diplomat from the nearby Land of Latecoming, once observed that the Land of Swallows enjoyed such an abundance of wild fruits and berries that its citizens could live for months on end without troubling themselves over farming and harvests. Such a comment, if anything more than a bit of political flattery, could reflect the tail-end of the prehistoric cornucopia that may have first attracted Peking Man to the region. Yan was the weakest of the seven states of the era, but its alliance was highly prized for the security it could offer for moving troops to other borders, contributing to war efforts and protecting the flanks of its neighbours.

It was widely believed, particularly among politicians,

that China was on the threshold of a new era. With the ancient lineage of the Zhou kings now exercising little power beyond the walls of its own capital, true power lay with their dukes. China was fated to enter another cycle of civil war, and after an indeterminate period of fighting, a single monarch would rise to subdue and unite the warring factions.

The Land of Swallows was spared much of the strife of the Warring States – the main culprit behind the wars of the fourth century BC was the distant Land of Qin, which dared not send an army against the Land of Swallows for fear that other countries would use the opportunity to attack it from the rear. Over the years, however, the men of Qin won battle after battle, and as the borders of the distant state expanded, they grew ever closer to the Place of Thistles.

Intrigues of the Warring States

Two countries were on a collision course. One was the aforementioned Land of Qin, a harsh regime in the west, run on military lines and geared for permanent war. The other was Qi, the Land of the Devout, directly to the south of the Land of Swallows, determined to become the over-lord of the assembled kings – the word for such a ruler, *ba*, weirdly endures today as part of the Chinese term for a Big Mac, a *ju wu ba*, or 'tyrant without compare'.

During the fourth century BC, the dukes of China cast off their loyalty to the powerless kings of the Zhou dynasty. Instead, each proclaimed himself a king in his own right. Duke Yi (r. 332–321) proclaimed that the Land of Swallows was no longer a vassal domain, but a fully independent state. For the last two years of his reign, he was not a duke, but Beijing's first king, and his bold proclamation ushered in 101 years of monarchy.

Despite their claims of independence, most of the rulers of the former dukedoms entertained some hope that they would not merely prosper themselves, but dominate over the others. They sought not to forget the Zhou kings of old, but to become just like them, absorbing their neighbours through means fair or foul, until one single autocrat dominated All under Heaven. The victor in that century of struggle would be the distant Land of Qin to the west, the homeland of Duke Yi's wife. Cut off in its own remote valley, the state of Qin nurtured a project that was literally decades in the making, designed to create the perfect ruler, a ruthless conqueror devoid of any thought but domination, ruling an unstoppable state run on harsh and military discipline. The culmination of that bloodline would be born in 246 BC and is remembered as the First Emperor of China. But in the hundred years that would pass before his victory over the Warring States, the other kingdoms jockeyed among themselves.

Even though it was stuck in its obscure corner, the Land of Swallows was soon embroiled in intrigues that characterised the period. With the death of its first king, his mourning period was not even officially over before the Land of Swallows was attacked by the neighbouring Qi, Land of the Devout, in a swift raid that seized ten cities on the countries' mutual borders. The diplomat Su Qin was immediately dispatched as an envoy to the Land of the Devout, where he offered his congratulations to the king and, in the same breath, his condolences.

The king of the Land of the Devout was not expecting such a response, and he pursued the ambassador across the throne room with a spear, demanding an explanation. Fearlessly, Su Qin told his enemy of what might happen. The Land of Swallows was indeed weak, but its marriage alliance with Qin gave it a friend in need – the leader of the most powerful and fearful army in the known world. The Land of Devout had snatched territory from its neighbour, engulfing it like a starving man grabs for food, but Su Qin warned his enemy that the territory he had just taken would turn out to be more like a deadly poison for the enemy who devoured it.

The story we have is from the *Intrigues of the Warring States*, a book emphasising the wily nature of diplomatic discourse. But Su Qin's dialogue with the Land of the Devout is wholly believable. It was enough to make the Land of Devout return the territory, pay extensive damages and offer a profound apology to both the Land of Swallows and its Qin allies.

Su Qin's younger brother Su Dai performed a similar role for King Kuai (r. 320–314 BC). He, too, hoped to maintain the position of the Beijing region through intrigues, not military might. Su Dai was easily the match of his brother in such intrigues, and a consummate salesman, unafraid to put the tricks of pedlars and merchants to use in a courtly context. He was particularly fond of an old parable about a man trying to sell a fine horse, who stood, frustrated, in a marketplace for three days, without attracting any attention.

For Su Dai, the quality of the horse might be of importance in a battle, or in a race, but it would not necessarily attract buyers in a market. The man in the parable eventually paid someone to shill for him, loudly 'noticing' the horse, praising its attributes, and lamenting that he wished he had the money to buy it, in order to attract actual customers. It was this sales trick that Su Dai was determined to put to use on potential rivals in the Land of the Devout.

When the Land of the Devout 'invited' minor Yan royals to visit, Su Dai advised his ruler to send them willingly – they might be hostages in all but name, but they would also be long-term guests, more liable to form friendships and political connections than to make enemies. Su Dai suggested that this would be even easier if Yan supplied the visitors with gold, silver and fine artefacts, so that they could bribe, impress and cajole their hosts.

The *Intrigues of the Warring States* record Su Dai's plans paying off in several diplomatic coups. Once, before arriving in the Land of the Devout for an important summit, he directly asked a Qi official if the man would play the part of the eager horse-buyer, planting stories and praises of Su Dai's greatness in the court, ready to make his arrival all the more impressive. Of course, Su Dai offered to pay his new-found friend's expenses, offering him a thousand measures of gold as 'horse's fodder'.

But ultimately Su Dai's prime loyalty was to himself, and his machinations would cause trouble for the Land of Swallows, particularly regarding his brother-in-law Zizhi, on behalf of whose promotion he was happy to play the part of the overexcited horse trader. Thanks to Su Dai and Zizhi, the Land of Swallows became a laughing stock among the Warring States, as the site of a supposed experiment in enlightened government, which ended in disaster.

The aging King Kuai lasted barely six years before he decided to abdicate his position – possibly through a combination of bad omens, bad luck and bad advice. Like many ministers during the Warring States era, Zizhi prized the message of an ancient folk tale, in which the Yellow Sovereign's great-great-grandson decreed that the ideal person to take over his kingdom was not his biological heir, but his wisest minister. With the help of Su Dai, Zizhi persuaded the old king that the way to score the ultimate publicity coup against the Land of Devout, to shame them for all eternity and blind them with virtue, was to nominate Zizhi as his heir.

The other countries, it was argued, could not fail to be impressed with the Land of Swallows, whose ruler would become the first in recorded history to directly emulate the sage-kings of legend. Just as they had held off military might with words, surely such a decision would put them ahead in the race to be recognised as the rightful ruler of the world?

King Kuai had his doubts, but was assured that this, too, was another ruse. Zizhi pointed out that all the main ministers were supporters of the crown prince, and that of course, behind the scenes, the crown prince would still wield real power. The appointment of Zizhi as the new king would simply be an exercise in showmanship, for the greater good of the Land of Swallows.

It was a disaster. No sooner had King Kuai abdicated,

Zizhi and his supporters did just as they pleased. Their power-grab lasted for barely three years before it was confronted with a mass uprising, not just by members of the general population, but also a large faction within the army, unsurprisingly in cahoots with the dispossessed crown prince.

While the rival factions were fighting each other, the wily Land of the Devout saw its chance, and sent its own army unopposed across the border. By the time the dust had settled, the usurpers were dead, but much of the Land of Swallows was under enemy occupation. After another year, the neighbouring Zhao, Land of Latecoming, living up to its name, sent in its own forces, chasing out the invaders and placing the hapless prince on the throne as King Zhao (r. 311–279 BC).

King Zhao had become the ruler of a land in ruins and would never forgive the Land of the Devout for its opportunism. Nor was he particularly enamoured with the Land of Latecoming, a vassal state of distant Qin. An earlier ruler of the Land of Latecoming had assassinated a rival by smashing his skull in with a specially designed drinking goblet. It was, consequently, something of a racial stereotype that men of the Land of Latecoming were untrustworthy, two-faced brutes that were guaranteed to have ulterior motives. As King Zhao's new advisers saw it, his only hope of holding off an unwelcome return by his 'allies' from the Land of Latecoming was to go over their heads and contract an official alliance with his former enemy in Qin.

Another tale of the Warring States era credits Su Dai with the invention of a famous Asian folk tale. He claimed to have seen a large mussel on the banks of the river that marked the border between the Land of Swallows and the Land of Latecoming. The mussel was attacked by a heron and retaliated by slamming its shell shut, trapping the heron's beak. While the two animals remained locked in a stalemate, a passing farmer was able to catch them both. Su Dai likened the doubtful set-up of his fable to the constant warring of the minor states and warned that Qin would be the sneaky farmer who stood to benefit from the strife.

King Zhao's long reign was characterised by a single project – his desire for revenge against the Land of the Devout. Ultimately, he would oversee the organising of a coalition which would pulverise the Land of the Devout in 284 BC, invading on the flimsy pretext that the Land of the Devout had attacked an obscure statelet to its south. Unsurprisingly, its king had supposedly done so at the urging of a belligerent minister who had been bribed to suggest it by agents of the Land of Swallows!

The Land of the Swallows became a nominal partner in an international coalition, captured the enemy capital and brought home the greatest prize imaginable. The Great Regulator bell was an item of great magical power, property of the kings of old, and said to confer universal kingship on whoever possessed it. Along with several other mythical artefacts, the Land of the Devout had acquired it as part of the preparations for conquering all rival kingdoms. Now it was taken back to the Land of Swallows, and sat in King Zhao's palace.

This gathering of the great and good, however, did not long outlast King Zhao himself, whose death in 279 BC was followed by purges and conspiracies that caused many of his greatest ministers and generals to flee to other countries. King Hui (r. 278–272 BC) soon admitted his failings in a pleading letter to the exiles, begging for forgiveness, citing unfamiliarity with his new responsibilities and a mistaken trust in his officials.

A better class of king might have served Yan better, but the last ruler of the dynasty did not learn from past mistakes. King Xi (r. 254–222 BC) repeated the errors of his ancestors. To the west, the state of Qin's rolling conquest reached a terrifying height in the neighbouring Land of Latecoming, with a crushing defeat followed by a mass execution of literally hundreds of thousands of prisoners of war. Instead of regarding it as the portent that it undoubtedly was, all King Xi seems to have thought about was the opportunity this afforded him to invade his ruined neighbour.

King Xi was ready for war, but his general refused to consider an invasion even if his allotted troops were tripled in number. The angry king went ahead without the general and was forced to apologise after the well-trained and battle-hardened survivors of the earlier massacre were able to repel the invasion.

The Plot to Kill a King
Despite dynastic marriages that had ensured the rulers of the Land of Swallows and the Land of Qin were cousins of some description, the agents of Qin were still determined to conquer the known world. As the counts of the borderlands had been elevated to dukedoms, and then claimed kingship for themselves, one king was determined to proclaim

himself as the ruler of All Under Heaven. Regardless of family ties, the Land of Swallows risked being engulfed by the armies of Qin. Beset by famine in his own country, still suffering the shame of an embarrassing defeat in another quarrel abroad, King Xi was to be the last monarch of the Land of Swallows.

Tragically, King Xi had one of the best advisers of all. His own son and heir, Prince Dan, had actually been raised in Qin as one of the hostage-guests of the distant land. He had seen Qin's war machine at work first-hand and had been a childhood friend of the man who had become Qin's ruler. King Xi, it seems, was content to replay the endless cycle of invasion and counter-attack, of insult and apology, which had characterised centuries of the Warring States. The king of Qin was playing an altogether different game, determined to proclaim himself as China's First Emperor.

More than two thousand years after the events described, it is difficult to assign blame. Possibly, King Xi was far more concerned about Qin than he cared to admit, but was placed in a position of plausible deniability by his own staff. But, according to the historical record at least, King Xi had no part in the final solution of the Land of Swallows. Supposedly taking matters into his own hands, Prince Dan began a top-secret project to put a suicidal assassin with a poisoned dagger into the king of Qin's throne room. The assassin, a man called Jing Ke, lived for several years at the height of luxury and debauchery in the Land of Swallows, collecting, as it were, his payment in advance since he was unlikely to be alive to spend it afterwards.

Eventually, Jing Ke was dispatched to the Land of Qin,

travelling undercover as an ambassador. Behind him, the entertainers, servants and enslaved girls who had attended to him for so many months were already dead, along with many of Prince Dan's trusted and devout agents, killed to prevent the secret plan coming out.

Jing Ke and his henchman were almost successful. After years of planning, months of travel and days of waiting for the perfect moment to strike, he got close enough to the king of Qin to snatch at his sleeve, leaping at him with the dagger, which he had kept hidden in a rolled-up map. But the king evaded his would-be killer, and the mission was a failure.

Jing Ke's mission has achieved legendary status in the centuries since. His ill-fated murder attempt was the last thing that stood between the days of feudal China and the initiation of the imperial era, for the king he failed to kill would soon become the First Emperor. But there is something strange about the mission. If it were that secret, how do we know about it?

Jing Ke did not make it out of the king of Qin's throne room alive. He died slumped against a pillar, struck repeatedly by the king with a massive ceremonial sword. Possibly, the story of the plot was extracted by torture from his henchman, whose fate is not recorded in the history books. But otherwise, the allegation that Prince Dan initiated the project is merely circumstantial.

Whether or not it was truly a top-secret plot by Prince Dan, Jing Ke's brief scuffle with the king of Qin was to spell the end of the Land of Swallows. Using the assassination attempt as a pretext, the army of Qin launched an assault on the Land of Swallows, using the Land of Latecoming as a staging post. By 226 BC, the capital of Yan had been occupied by Qin troops, and the last king of the Land of Swallows had fled to the north-east. Although fighting continued for several more years, the state of Yan was no more. King Xi appeased Qin by handing over a suitable scapegoat – Prince Dan's head was sent to Qin, and, soon after, King Xi himself surrendered.

The Land of Swallows was gone, along with all the other states. All Under Heaven was now unified in a single political entity, ruled by the First Emperor. China was born.

2

North and South: 221 BC–AD 1215

The place itself, and the meaning underlying it, is just over a thousand years old. The first building of its type in Beijing was built here in Ox Street in AD 996, although there is very little left of that first incarnation. It was destroyed by the Mongol invasion (see Chapter 3), entirely rebuilt in the Qing dynasty (see Chapter 4), and the area around it was thrice renovated in the twentieth century. The final change – for some, the final indignity – came in 2002, when the area around it was substantially 'improved', gentrified and de-cluttered to make a wider public space.

To the incautious observer, it might look like just another temple, but there are clues that this one is different. Compass in hand, you might notice that this does not face south like a Buddhist temple, but west towards a famous city far removed from China. There are, notably, no statues – the people who worship here have no truck with symbolic representations of human form. They have lived here for a thousand years – there are more than twenty million of them in China, forming such a prominent minority that they once had their own stripe on the Republican flag. The men are often darker-skinned than the average Beijinger and clad in small white hats, the women often veiled. Their shops sell mutton and *laghman* noodles, plum juice and Middle-Eastern candies.

Walk inside, and you are greeted by the black-bricked tombs of famous imans, and a cursive script that proclaims: 'There is no God but Allah, and Muhammad is his Prophet.'

what had once been the Land of Swallows became a mere administrative district. The earthen rampart to the north of the Place of Thistles was strengthened and lengthened, eventually linking up with similar ramparts in the Land of Latecoming to form the first incarnation of China's Great Wall.

The Land of Swallows was never truly a kingdom again, although later centuries occasionally raised ghosts of the past. A generation later, within a few months of the fall of the First Emperor's son, a rebel in the region proclaimed that the Land of Swallows lived once more. He was killed by another usurper, and within a couple of years the resurgent kingdom had been reincorporated into the empire. The Land of Swallows reappeared again in AD 27, when the local prefect briefly enjoyed two years as a self-crowned ruler. For much of the early Christian era, the ruler of the region enjoyed the status of a king (*wang*), although the meaning of the title had been devalued in imperial China, becoming more equivalent to a prince. Western China, closer to the new imperial capital at Luoyang, was ruled in a system of prefectures and provinces. Eastern China, including the Beijing area, was less tightly controlled and often enjoyed a status more akin to tributary princedoms.

China's former kingdoms have never been forgotten. Throughout the imperial era, they lingered in poetic allusions and administrative divisions; in modern times, they endure in odd places: as brand names for local products, and even as the provincial designations on some car number plates. Chinese astrologers divided the sky itself into nine areas, each believed to be a heavenly parallel with its earth-bound equivalent – activity in the Yan quadrant, be it meteors or supernovae, was sure to be tallied with troubles in the area marked by the former borders of the Land of Swallows.

Beijing as a Borderland

At some point, the region was inundated with seawater once more, turning hundreds of square miles into marsh-land. Just one of many changes in local features, the flood led to the rechristening of the area as *Kuhai*, the Bitter Sea, and to local stories that blamed the problem on those angry local dragons, unwilling to allow human settlers into their domain. The mischievous spirits were usually depicted as a family of four – the dragon king and his wife, son and daughter – and town planning in Beijing remained domi-nated by concerns of ensuring an adequate water supply.

Despite this, the region prospered, attracting foreign immigrants such as the Xianbei, who settled in the Beijing area and refused to budge. Chinese historiography before the twentieth century had a habit of writing off all immi-grants as 'barbarians' – conveniently forgetting the insult just as soon as the new arrivals had married into local fami-lies, adopted Chinese names and settled down. Many parts of what is now called China were home to unique civilisa-tions distinct from that of the 'Han' Chinese, but centuries of contact have diminished their local qualities. Today, there are but a few indicators of what were once very different cultures, such as the forked swords and alien statues of the native Sichuanese; the blunted, blocky pagodas that remain in the domain of the Xixia; the prominent Western noses of the descendants of Persian refugees in the hinterland; or the differing costumes and Muslim faith of the inner Asian Uyghurs. Similar cultural contacts appear to have been a feature of the Beijing region, where the local military developed a reputation for proficient cavalrymen, thanks largely to recruits from 'barbarian' immigrant communities like the Xianbei.

There are moments in the records where we can see the alien nature of Beijing life showing through. In the first century BC, three local men approached a magistrate from the south in a paternity dispute. The magistrate was aghast to discover that the three men all had the same wife, and scandalised when he realised that they had sought his aid because they had assumed he would regard their arrangement as completely normal. There were four children of this ménage, and the case turned on the question of who was whose. The magistrate observed that such questions of paternity and inheritance were precisely why Chinese tradition demanded a man should have a single wife or, at worst, a chief wife and many concubines. There was simply no provision in Chinese tradition for a single woman with many husbands, and such polyandry was regarded as a barbaric affront to Chinese decency. The shocked magistrate therefore ordered the execution of the offending husbands, regarding their behaviour as 'inhuman'.

Whether the ruler was a prefect or a governor, a prince or a 'king', he was powerful enough to bring major changes.

The Bitter Sea was brought back under control, with a network of canals dug for proper irrigation. Some of the worst of the marshes were drained in public projects that clearly benefited all. When an earthquake in AD 294 damaged the network, everybody pitched in on repairs – even the Xianbei, regarded by the central government as unwelcome immigrants.

Perspectives, of course, differ. For many generations of Chinese emperors, the Beijing region remained a borderland, perilously close to the wild north, open to assault by any number of external tribes. But life looked different in Beijing itself, where the 'barbarians' were not a haunting, unknowable threat, but often relatives, trading partners, in-laws and friends. In what would become a feature of Beijing life for over a thousand years, the region enjoyed a dual status, not just as a north-eastern outpost of 'traditional' Chinese civilisation, but as a south-eastern centre for the outlying tribes. Not all were fierce nomads on horseback, although many were. To the layman, it would be extremely different to tell a Beijing barbarian from a Beijing Chinese – they ate the same food, wore the same clothes and argued about the same things.

For a sense of this largely forgotten element of northeast Asian culture, you need only go to a Russian restaurant and ask for 'Siberian dumplings'. It is something of a shock when one's order arrives, comprising objects indistinguishable from Chinese *jiaozi*, lacking only Chinese condiments. The dumpling travelled both east and west from Central Asia in the early Middle Ages, along with the durum wheat that was a vital component of both it and noodles – neither is native to China, and yet both are commonplace on Chinese menus, particularly in 'Peking' restaurants. Rice remained relatively unpopular in the north until at least the end of the first millennium – paddy fields used up far greater quantities of precious water than the administration could really afford, while the largely cavalry-based military complained that the boggy ground proved difficult for their squadrons to cross at speed. Even today, rice from China's north-east is a rarity – highly regarded and priced at a premium, not least because the northern climate only permits a single crop per year.

For a brief period in the AD 300s, the ruler of the Land of Swallows was once more able to claim that he was indeed a true king, but this sign of the wavering of imperial authority carried implications of its own. The emperor's power was failing beneath incursions from new western barbarians, and when these attackers reached Yan, its renewed independence was crushed beneath a new imperium.

The Ballad of Mulan

We see traces of this new culture in one of China's most famous poems, the *Ballad of Mulan*. Known today chiefly for its use as inspiration for the Disney film, our modern image of Mulan is based on riotously anachronistic artistic licence. Style in the 1998 cartoon often leans on Han-dynasty carvings, whereas the Beijing depicted in the film's finale owes much of its architecture to the Qing dynasty. But Mulan's tale probably dates from the fifth or sixth century of the Christian era, when north China was under barbarian control.

Presented at first like a poem of lost love, it shows a girl sighing at her loom, only to reveal, to the great surprise of many a tavern audience, that she is not pining from unrequited love, but from a desire to do her family proud by joining the army.

> Last night I saw the army notice .
> The khan calls up the soldiers
> Conscription lists in twelve scrolls
> And each one names a father.

Since Mulan is an only child, there is no brother to take her father's place in the conscription rolls, and she resolves to disguise herself as a man and join up herself. But the magic word here is 'khan', not 'emperor'. Although Mulan later meets him in person, and he is described later in more traditional terms as the 'Son of Heaven', the man with whom she is dealing is clearly not a traditional Chinese ruler. She serves ten years in a prolonged campaign, in locations as far afield as the Yellow River and the 'Mount of Swallows', before a grateful khan offers her a government position.

> The khan asks for her desire [but]
> Mulan has no need of high office,
> 'Just a sturdy camel
> To take me to my distant home.'

The world in which the original Mulan serves is so alien to traditional China, so caught up in the Inner Asian worldview, that her mount of choice is a camel – this is usually forgotten in depictions of her, which, if they show her with a steed, show her with a horse. And yet, she lives in a society advanced enough for her 'barbarian' town to possess four markets (a stylised description in verse five describes her shopping for her equipment) and organised enough to have roll-calls of conscripts. It is far removed from the Mulan of the Disney cartoon, who is shown *defending* China from such northern barbarians, who have climbed over the Great Wall to threaten the south.

Buddhism had also spread into China from India, and the new religion proved particularly popular among the northern tribes. In part, this may have been because they too saw themselves as new arrivals, but Buddhism also offered an escape route from the homespun, relentlessly parochial concerns of Chinese folk religion. This became particularly important in the early Middle Ages. China was reunited under the Sui emperors, who immediately flung their nascent realm's limited resources into a foreign war with the Koguryo kingdom of northern Korea – indeed, one modern retelling of the tale of Mulan suggests that she went on to fight in *that* war. In the Chinese fancy that life will imitate art, Beijing was renamed Youzhou, the Tranquil City, and functioned as the headquarters for a series of northward campaigns in the sixth and seventh centuries. The first campaigns were disastrous for China and caused religious friction between Chinese popular religion and the Buddhism of the new aristocracy. Chinese folk beliefs held that the best possible life was lived at home, in harmony and tranquillity, and that a peaceful new existence awaited in the afterlife if one's corpse was safely returned to its hometown, buried with full honours and appeased with regular ceremonial attention by one's ancestors.

This belief presented ample opportunity for religious dissent over the foreign wars of the new Sui emperors. Major defeats in Korea brought the Sui generals home, ready to fight another day, but they left many thousands of their soldiers for dead on foreign fields, without proper burial and with no hope of being transported home for the correct religious ceremony. The public backlash was a contributing factor to the swift demise of the Sui, over-thrown by their cousins, the Tang dynasty, within a single generation.

Determined to avenge the Korean defeat, the Tang emperor Taizong arranged for Beijing to gain its first ceno-taph in 645, the Temple of the Origin of the Law (*Fayuan-si*), where it was promised that monks would say prayers for the many war dead of the earlier campaigns. The founding of the temple was just one of several public relations exer-cises designed to bring the people around, but it failed to bring much luck to Taizong's armies. Fought to a standstill in Korea, he returned home a broken man. His successors were careful to appease both Buddhist and local beliefs, leading to several confusions. The most famous is probably the claim by the Empress Wu, who was a teenage concu-bine at the time of Taizong's death, that she was the earthly reincarnation of a Buddhist deity. But the clash of such dif-ferent religious beliefs would also create new myths, one of which became part of Beijing's rich heritage.

The Life and Death of Nezha

Buddhism brought with it a menagerie of new gods and demigods, picked up during the religion's spread through India, and co-opting many old Hindu deities into its pantheon. By the time Buddhism arrived in China, translation into and out of at least one foreign language, if not two, had wrought serious shifts in the interpretation of many scriptures. The snake- and elephant-inspired *naga* creatures of Hindu myth were transformed in translation into Chinese as *long*, or 'dragons', creating a tidal wave of new dragon stories to confuse local folk tales.

These 'dragon' legends became mingled with a local story about a trickster god, to create a myth that became permanently interwoven with Beijing folklore. In the days before Chinese children were entertained by legends of the Monkey King, they heard about a child with superpowers. After a long gestation period, Nezha was born to humble parents at an inauspicious hour of the morning. Cut from a fleshy sac by his father, the boy had three heads, each with a bonus central eye. He had eight hands, each wielding a golden weapon, and his whole body shone with an eerie red glow. Nezha could travel at great speed by riding on fiery wheels, and wielded a magic bracelet that could crush foes with the force of the entire horizon. Although some myths of Nezha appear to date from the second millennium BC, many seem to have been fashioned in medieval times. Suggestions, for example, that he was the shield-bearer to the ruler of Heaven, the Jade Emperor, probably date from the 800s, when the Jade Emperor was adopted as the patron deity of the Tang dynasty's ruling house.

One of the most famous tales about Nezha records his conflict with a local dragon, who took exception to the churning of the river waters while Nezha was doing his laundry. A boundary dispute soon turned into an argument about who really ruled the area's all-important water, and ended with Nezha lifting his magic bracelet (usually depicted as something more like a metal hoop) and slaying the dragon with a single blow. The other dragons demanded restitution, leading to a feud between Nezha's exasperated family and the all-powerful creatures. Eventually, Nezha took his own life to save his parents from having to pay any reparations, but his troubles continued in the afterlife. His mother built a temple to his memory, hoping thereby to ensure that he would be reincarnated – a Buddhist ending, tacked on a Chinese folk tale. His angry father, still intensely irked with his son's wild life and ignominious death, tore the temple down, leading a local priest to fashion a new Nezha out of lily stalks and lotus leaves. Eventually, the spirit of Nezha would be given a military post in Heaven, and there the confused story should end.

However, over the centuries, the story of Nezha came to be associated specifically with the Beijing region, particularly in the later days of the Ming dynasty, when Nezha would offer supernatural aid to the city's architects. Although the location of the original stories seems sited in some vague dreamtime, the drift of the imperial family, Chinese religion and straightforward population numbers towards the north-east led many to assume that Nezha's story was bound to be associated with Beijing. But such assumptions would have to wait until the day that China was united once more.

South, Middle and Holy Capital

For the four hundred years until 1368, Beijing was barely part of China at all. Its history went on, its trade continued, it stayed on the map, but its rulers were 'barbarians'. At the end of the Tang dynasty in 907, Khitan Tartars took control of north China, and Beijing with it. During this period, the ruins of the Great Wall defended the region from nobody. Nor was Beijing in the 'north' – in fact, in 938 it was renamed Nanjing ('south capital') in recognition of its relation to other urban centres of the Liao dynasty – a ruling elite of Khitan tribesmen. Putnam Weale wrote:

> [The Khitans] were a cheerful people, with a peculiar
> sense of humour and a still greater conviction of the
> inferiority of women. To show their contempt for
> them, it is still recorded that they used to slit the back
> of their wives and drink their blood to give them
> strength.

Chinese history books of this period usually claim that China was under the rule of the Song dynasty, but while 'real' Chinese history bumbled along in the south, and the emperors of the Song continued to call themselves the rulers of All Under Heaven, Beijing changed hands once more. Its new masters, in 1115, were a second Tartar tribe, the Jurchens, ('uncouth barbarians who soon drank themselves to death and destruction', observes Weale) who ruled as the Jin ('golden') dynasty until 1260, when they were ousted by still a third group of barbarians, the Mongols.

The names of the city continued to fluctuate. It was the south capital of the Liao, but was extensively enlarged and improved under the Jurchen, renamed the 'holy capital', Shengdu, and then the 'middle capital', Zhongdu – a fair indication of the successful advance by the Jurchen armies, who marched as far south as the Yangtze.

China is a pragmatic civilisation. It works its magic on its oppressors, and it has time to do so. If Peking Man could exist for millennia in his caves, it took a blink of an eye for the Chinese system to ensorcell its conquerors. The first days of any conquest were surely violent and dangerous, but within a few years, temptations were there to appeal to a ruler's sense of snobbery and self-worth. Chinese princesses reared the next generation of half-Tartar heirs, and the new rulers inherited a bureaucracy dominated by Chinese. Even if the belligerent conquerors had wanted to lose themselves in administration, there would never be enough of them to go round. Despite their unquestioned military might and the unavoidable fact of their dominance, they still felt dwarfed by the cultural and historical heritage of the land they had conquered. It was not enough for them to rule this little piece of China; they wanted the whole thing, and it did not take long at all for them to hear of the Mandate of Heaven. If they wanted to gain Heaven's blessing for their planned conquest of the south, they would have to behave in a Chinese manner. Although the conquerors planned on clinging to their own religion, they were soon dragged into the seasonal cycle of the Chinese world, making sacrifices at the altars of Heaven and Earth, Sun and Moon. Tellingly, Beijing did not even possess such important sacred spaces – the Jurchen had to build them themselves, in imitation of those that they knew could be found far to the south in 'real' China.

Beijing's new masters had an inferiority complex about the 'true' Chinese capital to the south, ruled by the emperors of the Song. Accordingly, they enlisted the services of Zhang Hao, a Chinese architect, to turn the city of Zhongdu into a Chinese-style capital that outdid the real thing. The Song capital of Kaifeng had grown organically over the centuries. It had developed suburbs beyond the walls, and strange kinks in its shape due to natural landmarks. Compare that to Beijing under the barbarians: almost a perfect square, oriented on a north–south axis in perfect keeping with the stipulations of ancient tradition.

The designs and sacred buildings of Jurchen Beijing were deliberately designed to recall the idealised chronicles of the forgotten capital of the kings of the Zhou Golden Age. By 1153, the 'barbarian' ruler of the Jurchen was worshipping in a Chinese style at altars built to ancient designs, and keeping Chinese-style ancestral tablets in order to pay homage to his forebears' spirits in special shrines.

He also adhered to Chinese superstitions. Although some temple pagodas might climb higher than a couple of stories, 99 feet was usually regarded as the maximum height allowable by the principles of feng shui. Good spirits, supposedly, flew through the air at a height of 100 feet, and any buildings in their airspace might impede the bestowal of fortune. As with so many explanations from Chinese geomancy, one is tempted to reverse cause and effect. It is, after all, far better to have the spirit world as an alibi, than it is to admit to a keen ruler that the tall buildings he wants in his own honour run the risk of collapse, earthquake damage and diminishing returns regarding their inhabitability in a pre-elevator age.

The Bridge of Magpies

Beijing under non-Chinese occupation also saw the reassessment of certain old legends, such as that of Draught Ox, a straight line of three stars in what we would call the constellation of Vega, and the Weaver Maid, a triangle of stars in what we would call the constellation of Altair. Although the constellations were two of many in the ancient Chinese sky, the fact that an ox-drover was usually male and a weaver female, and that the two stars were separated by the 'river' of the Milky Way, led later centuries to append a tale of star-crossed lovers who would be able to meet only once a year, on the seventh day of the seventh month, when a bridge of magpies would form across the river that divided them. The story of the Draught Ox and the Weaver Maid took many centuries to develop, but became particularly popular during the period of Jurchen rule over Beijing. On the seventh day of the seventh month, courtiers in Jurchen Beijing would wear badges showing the magpie bridge, supposedly in homage to the traditional festival, although possibly also out of a deep-seated sense of separation from the rest of China, south of the Jurchen border, eternally waiting for a fantastical remedy.

During the period of Khitan and Jurchen domination,

Beijing's population seemed obsessed with other cities, particularly the life they imagined was going on far to the south, in a China that was not under foreign rule. Thoughts were on romantic idylls of an idealised, peaceful existence under the Song, or military schemes, eternally plotted and redrafted, for an eventual takeover. Chinese on both sides of the border speculated about reunification, and as the barbarian ruling class was diluted with increasing amounts of Chinese blood with every generation, the separation of these two Chinas seemed increasingly ludicrous. By the thirteenth century, the standoff between the Northern Jin and Southern Song was no longer a matter of a slow invasion, whose frontline had remained static for more than a century. Instead, it had become a contest between two rival dynasties for the favour of Heaven. North and South both strove to outdo each other in the ostentation of their religious services, and with their capitals' claims to be the Centre of the World. Such boasts were not made to each other in diplomatic communications, but directly to Heaven, in a constant struggle for a sign, some portent or astrological manifestation, that China would soon be unified once more. As part of this one-upmanship, the denizens of Beijing clung to their own ancient history, particularly Beijing's brief period as a monarchy, and the dimly remembered legends of ancient prominence. Even when the capital of China was far to the south, the people of the Beijing region still assured each other that the land where they lived and died had been the site of ancient clashes between gods and demons, and (ironically with some element of truth) where men had first walked the earth.

A folk tale of the period maintains a sense of yearning for a lost unity with the south, subtly buried beneath a traditional love story. The association of the area with the swallow continued, particularly with reference to the Terrace Where Swallows Muster, an earth mound in the countryside outside modern Beijing, where thousands of birds congregated each autumn. Flocks of swallows sufficient to darken the sky stayed in the area for a few days, before beginning their winter migration south, to Hainan and points beyond. The sight of the birds, however, eventually generated a legend of its own, redolent of tragic medieval romances, Grimm's fairy tales and even a touch of Oscar Wilde, in the story of a rich landlord's daughter.

As the story goes, Hongbao ('Ruby') was persecuted for her innocent friendship with the son of a poor man. Despite her protestations that Xiao Yan ('Little Swallow') was just a friend, the girl was ordered never to see him. Her carefree childhood play was curtailed as she reached marriageable age, and she was no longer permitted to go outside. Imprisoned indoors with nothing to do but embroider, she amused herself by occasionally ditching the flower patterns she had been provided in favour of small and exquisite thread birds, which she would drop out of the window as gifts for Little Swallow.

Her father hears her whispering 'Fly, swallow! Fly away!' and immediately assumes the worst. So might we, but centuries of fairy-tale retellings have reversed the likely truth of the tale – instead, we are told that one of her embroidered birds has come to life, and it is that which she is addressing. Her scandalised father, however, will not be persuaded, and instead bribes a local magistrate to exile Little Swallow far to the south on trumped-up charges.

As Ruby pines away for her lost beau, she is visited by a lone bird, returning from the distant tropical island and tweeting the worst news that she can imagine: that Little Swallow has died in exile. Ruby asks the bird to confirm by flying three times around her house, which it does. Ruby then cries herself to sleep, weeping tears of blood – standard Chinese hyperbole for misery, but here taken literally. When she inevitably dies of a broken heart, she is buried up on the earthen slope near her house – a place that soon grows with strange 'Swallow Grass', whose blood-red sap can be squeezed out and used to make dyes and cosmetic rouge. Thereafter, each year, the swallows return to the terrace and wait for two days in the vicinity of the grave, in case the spirit of Ruby has a message for them to take south to Hainan.

North and South would eventually be reunited, but not through any Chinese or supernatural agency. In the thirteenth century, the North was conquered by a new tribe of outsiders – the Mongols. Beijing put up a brave resistance to the approach of Genghis Khan – brave because the Mongols famously offered no quarter to any who refused to surrender. By not immediately opening its gates to the Mongols, Beijing sealed its own fate, and the city succumbed to a relentless storm of fire-arrows in 1215. The Mongols, their forces swelled by defecting Chinese soldiers who had originally been tasked with defending the city, crashed through the gates and put every living thing to the sword. The surviving palaces were looted and set on fire, and by the time the army had passed, Beijing had been totally destroyed.

A surviving report of the immediate aftermath paints a terrifying picture. The fires reduced the buildings of Beijing to charred ruins, while men, women and children had died in such huge numbers that the streets were slick with human fat. Beijing was left to the buzzards and remained a ghost town for several decades, until Khubilai, the grandson of Genghis Khan, completed the conquest of China, uniting the country for the first time in centuries, and proclaimed himself the first emperor of a new dynasty, which he gave the majestic and provocative title of Yuan – 'beginning'.

This new start solved the enduring problem of the rival capitals in North and South. The new ruler chose the location of the true capital. He chose Beijing.

3

Khanbalikh: 1215–1368

A short stroll west from Mudanyuan station (Line 10), by the side of the canal that once formed the moat of his city wall, there is an imposing statue of Khubilai Khan. He sits on a throne borne by four elephants, flanked by two lissome women in the crooked witches' hats favoured by his mother and wife, and accompanied by a lithe, alert leopard.

Khubilai himself is incredibly fat. His bulk is so huge that he leans on his left hand, buttressing his upper body as if keeping himself upright is a chore even when seated. This is the gout-ridden, morbidly obese tyrant of the historical record at the moment of his greatest triumph: the foundation of the city of Khanbalikh in 1271. Stretching away to either side of him is an intercultural parade of minions – his Arab astronomer, his Nepalese architect, a Buddhist monk and sundry other foreigners, to hammer home the message of the commemorative plaque in front, that the khan's great city was founded through the efforts of 'the people of all nations'. There is even a crucifix – a rare sight in China – sitting alone to one side in seeming recognition of his dabbling with foreign religions. It was after all, Khubilai who asked the Polo brothers to bring back great Christian minds to dispute with other religions at his court, so he could best decide which path to follow. Famously, they failed to turn up with any actual monks, but did lend him young Marco Polo as a servant.

Polo joined Khubilai's multicultural staff, alongside Uyghurs, Mongols and Jurchens, as well as the Chinese. One such local collaborator, Guo Shoujing (1231–1316), is largely unknown to foreigners, although his place in the history of Chinese science is unassailable. He is such a big deal that Beijing manages to have *two* statues of him – curious when one considers the propensity of governments to honour rulers and despots rather than the boffins who scurry to carry out their commands. But, then again, Guo Shoujing was Chinese, and Khubilai Khan was a Mongol invader.

A child prodigy in the latter days of the Song dynasty, Guo found his true niche in the wake of the Mongol conquest, when Khubilai Khan put him in charge of repairing Beijing's infrastructure. He oversaw the repair of the Grand Canal and the construction of an aqueduct to convey much-needed fresh water to the capital. In his fifties, collating data from dozens of observatories all around China, he reported on the true length of the year to the emperor. In his sixties, he was appointed as the head of governmental water works, bringing him into intimate contact with trade conduits and water supply issues. He was the most prominent scientist of Yuan-dynasty Beijing.

A broad head-and-shoulders bust of Guo can be found at his memorial pavilion at the far northern end of the Houhai lake, where his Baifu Canal once brought water 30 kilometres from the Baifu spring, through Kunming Lake at what is now the Summer Palace and into the centre of Khubilai's capital. He wears a scholar's cap, he has protruding ears and his lips are pursed through his goatee beard as if he is just about to voice his disapproval. If he seems a little angry, it might have something to do with the constant carping directed at his achievements – it is frequently suggested that much of his work in mathematics and astronomy had been ripped off from Muslim scholars at Khubilai's court, although nobody has ever managed to prove this.

A second, more modest bust of him can be found in the grounds of the Ancient Observatory, close to where his Tonghui Canal left the city to connect to the Grand Canal 17 kilometres away. The beard is longer here, but the scowl is still present.

In linking Beijing to the Grand Canal, Guo transformed the city, integrating the capital into the Chinese system, but also making it possible for there to be a capital at all. At the time of his birth, Beijing still lay largely in ruins. The Grand Canal was vital in making it possible not only for a city to function, but for the workmen and materials to reach the city in order to rebuild it in the first place.

The Chessboard Streets
When Khubilai Khan's architects began constructing what would be known as Khanbalikh, 'the khan's city', they ignored the blackened, haunted shell of the old town, and built a completely new one on its north-east corner. Marco Polo wrote that Khubilai's astrologers had predicted that the old town would rebel, and so encouraged him to weasel out of the curse by building *nearby* instead of *rebuilding* the site itself.

But while such folk tales may have made for amusing fireside anecdotes in local taverns, they ignored more prosaic reasons for the move. The ruined city could have easily been restored, but the Mongols were planning for a much bigger metropolis. Beijing had been the meeting place of North and South for many centuries, but now Khubilai was to proclaim himself as a Chinese emperor, the first of the new Yuan dynasty, he would need more than just a regional capital. He needed a national nexus, and with such a plan came the expectation of a much larger urban population. Khubilai's city soon grew into one of the largest in the world, laid out with wide regular avenues that impressed all foreign visitors. The most famous contemporary account of the city is by Marco Polo, who wrote of the city of 'Cambaluc' in his *Travels*.

> All the plots of ground on which the houses of the
> city are built are four-square and laid out with straight
> lines; all the courts and gardens of proportionate size
> ... Each square plot is encompassed by handsome
> streets for traffic, and thus the whole city is arranged in
> squares just like a chess board ... In the middle of the
> city there is a great [bell] which is struck at night. And
> after it had struck three times, no one must go out of
> the city.

Polo was able to get a bird's eye view of the city by climbing the steps to the roof of one of the city's eleven gates (he counted twelve, but close enough). The city was smaller in those days, and smog-free, and Polo was able to see clear across to the opposite wall – the avenues were straight all the way.

The dragons of the Bitter Sea, those recurring characters of Beijing legend, would also have their say. The water supply for the old city was simply too paltry to support Khubilai's plans. It was far better for the Mongols to site their new capital on the north-eastern edge of the old town, where two rivers flowed into an elongated pair of lakes, the site of a previous royal park, before continuing on their way out of town. Khubilai's personal palace was built on the eastern shore of one of these lakes, which was dredged and expanded – the soil and rocks from the process dumped to the north to form the basis of what is now Coal Hill to the north of the Forbidden City.

One of the few remnants of the Mongol era survives in what is now Beihai Park where the serene and most northerly lake curves gracefully around Hortensia Island, once the private preserve of the Mongol emperors. Marco Polo described the park in its Yuan dynasty heyday as a paradise:

> Between the two walls of the enclosure are fine parks
> and beautiful trees bearing a variety of fruits. There
> are beasts also of sundry kinds, such as white stags and
> fallow deer, gazelles and roebucks, and fine squirrels ...
> There extends a fine Lake, containing fish of different
> kind which the Emperor has caused to be put there, so
> that whenever he desires any he can have them at his
> pleasures. A river enters this lake and issues from it, but
> there is a grating of iron or brass put up so that the fish
> cannot escape in that way.

Polo may never have seen the park for himself – or, if he did, it was only on a brief escorted visit. He does, however, have plenty to say about other pleasures on offer elsewhere in the city, and claims that Yuan-era Beijing boasted some 20,000 sex workers.

Place names and folklore retain vestiges of many a drunken night in Beihai Park. Several trees in the park were awarded ministerial rank in old imperial governments, doubtless by sozzled rulers. Although a bridge now connects Hortensia Island to the rest of the park, in Khubilai's time it was only reachable by boat. A day in the park would end with boating on the lake in the sunset, and at dusk all the barges would be moored at the island, and the khan and his followers could spend the night with their women in a number of exquisite pavilions. For any consort who had managed to run a gauntlet of obstructive eunuchs and imperial caprices, a night trapped on Hortensia Island was a coveted opportunity; for any Yuan-dynasty beauty who did not want the attentions of an amorous emperor, it was a night-long test of endurance.

The park was not always as tranquil as it seems today. Beijing folklore retains a tale that may be the vestiges of a forgotten murder or simply a groundless bogeyman to scare children. But, so the stories go, sometimes a black-cloaked man can be found in Beihai Park, offering to take late-night loiterers home. Instead of being a friendly old-world taxi driver with a donkey cart, the man is actually a ghost, determined to drag unsuspecting passengers down into his lair beneath the bridge, where he drowns them in the waters of the lake and feeds on their souls.

Resident in Beijing sometime in the 1280s, Polo was a *semuren* – a 'person of the various categories' – one of many hundreds of foreign administrators employed by the Mongols to aid in running their newly conquered country. Most of the *semuren* were from Central Asia, and their number included many Nestorian Christians and Muslims, leading to certain anxieties in the capital. Matters were particularly tense over the subject of religion – missionaries from all major faiths, as well as a number of cultists and outright charlatans, were honoured guests at Khubilai's court, and were kept permanently guessing as to the emperor's disposition towards them. All lived in hope that the Mongol conqueror would recognise their belief as the one ultimate truth, and drag the people of China along with him in his conversion. But Khubilai hedged his bets throughout his reign, refusing to come out for or against any one religion. His chief wife was a Nestorian Christian, most of his advisers Buddhists or Muslims, but Khubilai himself was careful to appeal to everyone.

The Tartar City

The Mongols dwelt in the newly built area or 'Tartar city', while the old ruins and the formerly unoccupied land filled up with their subjects – the ruins were not abandoned for long, but soon attracted entrepreneurs and merchants who wiped out most traces of the old city. Few Mongols and fewer of the foreign *semuren* administrators were fluent in Chinese, and most communications among Polo's colleagues were conducted in Persian. It seems that Polo himself never learned more than a few words of Chinese, leading to many supposed 'errors' in his account of his travels. In fact, his experience of China was akin to that of a foreign diplomat on a brief fact-finding mission, forced to regard everything through the limited opportunities afforded for actual local contacts.

The centuries of North–South divide in China had created palpable differences, enough for Polo to believe that China was two countries – 'Khitai', where Beijing was located, and 'Manzi' to the south. Ironically, the latter term was actually Chinese for 'southern barbarian', co-opted by the occupied North as a derogatory term for China proper. There are tantalising hints in Polo's account that someone sat him down on at least one occasion and attempted to explain how Beijing had been subject to non-Chinese rule for some time before the arrival of the Mongols. However, the story was easily garbled – determined to make themselves sound legitimate, the Jurchens had given their dynasty a Chinese name: Jin. As it literally means 'golden', Polo seems to have confused this period (1115–1234) with an unrelated Jin kingdom two thousand years previous, and the close pronunciation of Qin, the dynasty of the First Emperor. This caused him to relate fanciful and muddled tales of a legendary 'Golden King' in the region, that were linked, probably by his own wishful thinking, to other stories of the fabled Christian king of Asia, Prester John.

Polo's description of the khan's realm includes discussions of Muslim peoples, primitive tribes in the jungles, Indians, Tibetans and Turks. On rare occasions when Polo did deal directly with the Chinese themselves, he often found them infuriating – particularly the women, who were demure, graceful and entirely unavailable.

The most important development for Beijing during Polo's time was the renovation of its Grand Canal. At first, the Mongols expected that grain fleets sailing up the coast of China, into the Gulf of Bohai and then upriver near what is now Tianjin could feed Beijing's hungry mouths. Pirates aside, the greatest danger was the weather, which culminated in a disastrous sequence of events in the famine year of 1286 when a quarter of the city's grain was lost at sea in storms.

Partly out of a deep-seated mistrust of the open sea, and partly from a pragmatic desire to avoid pirates and charge enforceable tolls, the Mongols ordered the construction of a canal that would connect Beijing to the South. Khubilai made the renovation (in fact, recreation) of the old Sui-dynasty canal his top priority, and symbolically reunited North and South with a critical waterway for the first time in centuries. Chinese rulers had dredged river transportation corridors across the land before, but the Yuan dynasty saw a vast improvement. At the time of Polo's residence, the canal still stopped a way short of the metropolis itself, obliging merchants to offload their cargoes and wheel them the final few miles into Beijing on carts. Around 1293, shortly after Polo left China for his European homeland, the canal network was extended right to Beijing itself. It went up all the way to the east wall of the emperor's palace, and then around to the north, where it ended in a huge inland harbour, with ample docking facilities in the middle of the city. Some vestige of this Beijing 'port' survives today as the cluster of lakes at Houhai, now a picturesque district of bars and restaurants to the north of Beihai Park.

The canal made it possible for grain barges to come all the way to Beijing from the fertile South: from river system to lake to canal to river system, without once having to head for open water. It was now feasible to have a capital in the North that continued to grow – the Mongols had planned sufficiently ahead, and their new, larger water supply and better provisioning ensured that Beijing would grow swiftly.

The Marco Polo Bridge

Transport networks were improved elsewhere, too. To the west of Beijing, Polo described a bustling market, where a sturdy bridge complete with churning water mills became the site of a trading post – with merchants unloading their goods ready for trans-shipment, but often hoping to save on cargo by selling them off right away:

> When you leave the city … and have ridden ten
> miles, you come to a very large river which is called
> Pulisangkin and flows into the ocean, so that
> merchants with their merchandise ascend to it from the
> sea. Over this river there is a very fine stone bridge, so
> fine indeed that it has few equals.

The river was known as the Sanggan from the eighth century onwards, but this appears to be a coincidence. His *Pulisangkin* is not Chinese at all, but simply Persian for 'stone bridge'. The Chinese themselves called it the bridge of *Lugou* ('the Cottage/Black/Lu Family Waterway'), but today it is known outside China as the Marco Polo Bridge.

> The fashion is this: It is 300 paces in length and it must have a good eight paces in width, for ten mounted men can ride across it abreast. It has twenty-four arches and many water mills, and is all of a very fine marble, well built and firmly founded. Along the top of the bridge there is on either side a parapet of marble slabs and columns made in this way: at the beginning of the bridge there is a marble column, and under it a marble lion so that the column stands upon the lion's loins while on top of the column there is a second lion both being of great size and beautiful sculpture. At the distance of a pace from this column, there is another precisely the same, also with its two lions and the space between them is closed with slabs of grey marble to prevent people from falling over into the water. And thus the columns run from space to space along either side of the bridge, so that altogether it is a beautiful object.

In the twenty-first century, the Marco Polo Bridge has been carefully renovated. Some original paving slabs are retained in its central walkway, but for show only, so that modern visitors can gaze in awe at the wear and tear done to hard stone by centuries of footfalls from litter-bearers, porters and cutpurses. Stone friezes and statues at either end tell tales about the bridge's history, but they are clearly modern additions. So, too, are many of the stone lions that first attracted Marco's attention. One only needs to look at the heads of the giant stone turtles, worn almost featureless by generations of attention from excited children, to see how a true Yuan-dynasty artefact is likely to look today.

The Drum and Bell Towers

The period of Mongol rule saw the construction of drum and bell towers to match the city's expanded size. The absence of any form of readily available timepiece meant that the standard method of timekeeping across the city for merchants, priests and members of the public was defined by the sounding of the central towers. The drums were beaten in the morning to signify dawn, the bells rung at night to announce the formal end of the day – Beijing did not have a curfew as such, but anyone going out after the sounding of the bell tower would need a lantern to light their way, and a bodyguard to watch over them.

The Mongol Bell Tower was built in 1272, and stood for nearly five hundred years before its destruction by fire and replacement with the one that stands today. But it is the Mongol tower that became part of Beijing's local folklore, its huge bell producing a surprisingly mournful, soft chime each evening, sounding to Chinese ears like someone whispering *xie, xie*.

Beijing children were told that it was time to go to bed, because the Bell Goddess was calling for her shoe (*xie*), a story that grew with the telling to become a tragic fairy tale of the bell's construction. An unnamed emperor (presumably Khubilai) ordered his minister of works to cast a ten-tonne bell, but was displeased with the iron monstrosity that was first produced. He told his craftsmen to come up with a bronze replacement in just three months, big enough and loud enough for its sound to carry as far as Beijing's suburbs.

Working under pain of death, the craftsmen faced great difficulty with their enforced materials. It was possible for them to cast bronze at such a great size, but they were unable to guarantee the finished bell would ring true. As attempt after attempt met with dull, unsuitable chimes, the workmen began to lose heart. On the day before the deadline, the lead craftsman's daughter arrived at the foundry, clad in her best clothes, and asked how the work was coming along. On hearing that the situation was still desperate, she flung herself into the molten bronze. Her anguished father was left clutching nothing but a single slipper, as his daughter sank forever into the agonising hot metal. Her death, however, supposedly brought about a great change in the quality of the bronze, leading to a miraculously clear tone in the huge bell.

Despite such desperate measures undertaken to create the perfect capital, Khubilai did not find Beijing wholly to his liking. He spent the hot summer months away from his new capital, far to the north at his secondary residence in Shangdu, the 'Xanadu' of poetic legend. As for the Yuan dynasty itself, it flourished only briefly. The conquering Mongol vigour was soon vanquished by the temptations of China itself – even as Khubilai proclaimed himself emperor, he was adhering to his own upbringing, which had deliberately favoured a Chinese attitude.

The Yuan dynasty did not last quite as long as the

ancient Land of Swallows – Khubilai and his descendants were masters of Beijing for just under a century, from 1271 to 1368. Along with their conquests they inherited the same problems as their predecessors – the usual cycles of famine and plenty, health and plague. The Mongols changed China forever and reunited it after centuries of the North–South divide, but by the mid-1300s China was suffering from droughts and plagues that made it seem as if Heaven favoured another change in the ruler. An unidentified disease decimated the Chinese population in the 1330s, likely to have been the very same Black Death that would follow Mongol armies into distant Europe. The disease, or something similar, returned in an outbreak that killed millions between 1353 and 1354, exacerbating tensions among the survivors.

From the time of the first outbreak, the Mongol hold on China was slipping. Loyalties wore thin among the Chinese population that still greatly outnumbered their Mongol masters, and combined with superstition about the 'bad omens'. The simple struggle for survival did the rest of the job, leading to outbreaks of rebellion in the early- to mid-1300s. One of the rebel groups eventually grew to present an effective opposition to the Mongols, and successfully chased the Yuan dynasty rulers out of their 'khan's city'. As far at the Mongols were concerned, the Yuan dynasty continued for many more centuries, but the extent of its territory did not include China.

China, the 'khan's city' included, now fell under the leadership of a new 'dynasty of brightness' – the Ming. For a brief moment, it seemed as if Beijing would lose its old status, reverting to a peripheral town as the power base in China shifted back south. Instead, Beijing's position was strengthened and reaffirmed, almost by chance, and the city was rebuilt once more – improved beyond all recognition.

It was in the Ming dynasty that Beijing's all-important central citadel truly took its modern shape. Building on the start made by the Mongols, the new rulers of Beijing would refine their capital to create one of the most stupendous sights in the world – an entire city within a city, designed for the imperial masters, walled off from their subjects behind fortress walls, a centre of power designed and conceived to be the heart of the world itself, an axis about which the entire universe was expected to revolve.

4

The Forbidden City: 1368–1644

There is a long walk to his mausoleum. The metro station is some forty-two kilometres from the centre of town, and even then its name is Scenic Area for the Thirteen Tombs (*Shisan Ling Jingqu*). The visitor passes through several gates, and along a seven-kilometre road lined with statues of mighty beasts, scowling warriors and loyal scholars. The Thirteen Tombs stretch out in a semicircle in the foothills of the mountains to the north, a spread of temples with yellow imperial roofs, each set in maroon-walled enclosures like miniature versions of the Forbidden City.

His mausoleum is directly ahead of the approach road – every tomb has a Sacred Way approaching it, but you have just walked along the longest, for the greatest of the Ming emperors. Yongle, the Emperor of Perpetual Happiness (1360–1424), was the third of the Ming emperors, but the first to be buried in Beijing, his adopted capital. His bronze effigy dominates the main hall of his necropolis, seemingly in imitation of the throne he once occupied. He is thick-set, bearded, sitting with legs confidently wide apart, his hands resting on his thighs as if just about to issue a sternly worded decree. There is naked power coiled here, simmering in the air. His title is something of a misnomer; he was not happy with simply being a prince. He took the throne for himself, and moved his capital all the way north, dragging China's fortunes with it, for much of the next six hundred years.

Perpetual Happiness

The generation of warfare that led to the establishment of the Ming dynasty did considerable damage to Khanbalikh. The city had grown so large under the Mongols that it was unable to support itself without a stable country to keep its population fed. With the Grand Canal damaged by floods, silt and neglect, many in Khanbalikh had starved. The city's outlying regions were abandoned during the strife and plague; the old Mongol aristocrats were dead or exiled, and few Chinese seemed willing to seek out a place whose importance rested on now-discredited contacts with the peoples of the North and West. China's focus began to shift southward once more – Nanjing was now the capital, with Kaifeng in the West a subsidiary administrative hub.

Nanjing sat at the centre of rich and fertile plains, on a *real* river that was navigable far upstream – it needed none of the artificial watercourses or unstable supply routes of Khanbalikh. Its situation would allow it to grow much larger, and its location kept the new government closely linked to the loyal South, not the untrustworthy North.

With propagandist zeal and a smidgen of superstition, the old North capital was renamed Beiping, or Northern Peace, seemingly in the hope that harmony would prevail in the old Mongol heartland. The newly christened Northern Peace was not expected to fall into ruins. It was still a regional capital, and soon gained a princely patron whose influence would radically change the city's fortunes.

The first emperor of the Ming had twenty-six sons, most of whom were appointed as regional governors. Only the eldest was kept in the new capital; the rest were scattered across the empire and tasked with maintaining order in their father's name. The emperor's fourth son was given the north-east as his princedom, adopting the archaic title of Prince of Yan, in honour of the region's ancient past as the Land of Swallows. In the midst of empire-wide reconstruction, the newly arrived prince oversaw radical remodelling in the old Mongol capital.

Initially, he had no interest in restoring the city to its full glory. The canal was left derelict, and many of the old Yuan palaces were pulled down. The imperial city itself was reduced in size, its north wall moved southward, to create a more modest and manageable private area. Many of the old Mongol gardens were retained, but Coal Hill to the north now stood outside the imperial citadel proper.

Even though Chinese civilisation had supposedly been restored, it was impossible to expect a century of foreign rule to have left no mark. In the case of the Prince of Yan, growing up in a Mongol-ruled society seemed to impart certain expectations about the succession. With the death of his elder brother, the Prince of Yan began to assert that he, and not his young nephew, should be recognised as the rightful heir to the Ming emperor. It was a decidedly Mongol attitude towards the imperial succession, and one that the emperor was not prepared to allow. Before he eventually died in 1398, he expressly ordered his many surviving sons to stay away from the enthronement of his heir in Nanjing, for fear that they would attempt a coup.

Despite these admonitions, the Prince of Yan set out for Nanjing anyway, and was only thwarted when the army blocked his path. He returned, embarrassed, to the North, but the damage was already done. The Prince of Yan and his nephew would fight over the future of the empire in a three-year civil war, which ended with Nanjing in ruins, the nephew nowhere to be found and the administrative centre of the empire moved back north to the Prince of Yan's power base. Beijing had become the capital of all China, and would remain so until the present day, except for a brief period in the twentieth century.

The Prince of Yan, remembered in the dynastic histories as Yongle, the Emperor of Perpetual Happiness, was thus responsible for the rehabilitation of Beijing as an imperial capital, not only through his early reconstruction, but also for even more extensive rebuilding undertaken after his victory. It is said that Yongle stayed in the Beijing region out of a sense of military zeal – the hated Mongols were still at large, and he intended to personally lead the mop-up operations against them. But Beijing was also his personal fiefdom and the place where he was most likely to feel safe. There may have been Mongol enemies in the North, but Yongle cannot have placed much trust in his many disgruntled brothers or their expanding families in the South.

The Living God of Wealth

From 1406 to 1420, Beijing was a building site once more, its palaces being renovated, its lakes dredged and the grandeur of its Grand Canal restored. The Emperor of Perpetual Happiness faced strong resistance from his engineers;

many regarded the city as a doomed venture. Yongle's own minister of works dared to refuse the commission, reminding his ruler that the region was still widely regarded as the Waste of the Bitter Sea, and that the dragons of the area were too powerful to overcome. By 'dragons', the minister is likely to have meant the many unfavourable features of the terrain, but, to a casual reader, some of the court documents regarding the reconstruction can often seem as if Yongle were ordering his engineers to do battle with serpents and savage beasts.

The two imperial officers charged with redeveloping Beijing were legendarily at odds. Whether this is historically accurate or mere dramatic licence is unclear, but city folklore maintains that they sulked in separate quarters, each determined to prove the other to be a fool, only to be united in their town planning when both received the same vision – the ghost of a young boy, supposedly the spirit of Nezha himself, demigod of past dynasties, the suicidal multi-limbed child-hero who supposedly rode on fiery wheels and terrorised the local dragons. Nezha instructed each of them to 'copy' his own body. It is, so popular legend claims, this imitation of the eight-armed figure of Nezha that caused Beijing to have its Ming-dynasty layout.

Even when one has a Ming-dynasty city map, and not a later Qing-, Republican- or Communist-era street plan, the idea that the city is laid out in the shape of a giant god seems ludicrous. Geomancers have attempted lengthy discourses on the meaning of Beijing as a recumbent god, suggesting that a certain gate is an ear of Nezha; a certain pair of wells are his eyes; his feet rest on a pair of temples to the south; and the space in front of the Gate of Heavenly Peace is his lungs. And, since someone inevitably asks, his penis is thought to be the bridge that leads south from the Rear Gate. Even before the modern era, local inhabitants regarded such superstition with mild embarrassment, and not even the feng shui masters seemed to take it all that seriously. It is not the image of a god in Beijing's town planning that concerns the Chinese, it is the implication that, however the city was designed, a substantial element of its origin lay not in human artifice, but in divine inspiration.

The Ming-era reconstruction of Beijing comes accompanied by many other folk tales, from merry anecdotes of supernatural assistance to macabre tales of the grotesque. Yongle initiated an incentive scheme to encourage outlying provinces to aid the project – a decision which led to legends about the reconstruction of Beijing to spring up far from its actual location. In one case, it was said that the distant mountain Shenmu ('sacred trees') gained its name for the speed with which timber from the region had been floated down the Yangtze River, ready for shipment north to Beijing.

Since the Mongols left the city in a hurry, it was not a surprise that they left many of their possessions behind. Stories of Yongle's men pulling down Mongol palaces seem only partly born out from memories of demolition and renovation. Officers of the new regime were also likely to have been on the lookout for buried treasure, squirrelled away by the departed dynasty.

Folklore soon intervened, and the simple hunt for concealed bullion took on a legendary status, with stories of a man called the Living God of Wealth, blessed (or rather cursed) with the ability to find buried treasure. According to legend, the Living God of Wealth was an ordinary man with an extraordinary gift – somehow, he was able to simply know where valuable objects could be found. But after years of abuse from greedy bullies, he had taken on a hermit's existence, refusing to profit from his own knowledge, and choosing to live as a pauper.

It is likely that the story of a dirty, wretched tramp dragged before Ming officers and ordered to lead them to riches contains within it a more tragic tale – that of a loyal servant of the old regime, abandoned by his former masters and tortured by a new order hungry for monetary gain. Yongle ordered them to beat him until he took them to the treasure, and to beat him all the more if he turned out to be bluffing.

Before long, the bleeding, pleading form of the Living God of Wealth brought his tormentors to a patch of waste ground, and told them to dig. Beneath the surface they found ten secret vaults, containing nearly half a billion taels of silver. This, we are told, is the origin of the strangely named Ten Vaults Lake (Shichahai), which formed when the great hole in the ground eventually filled up with water. This folkloric explanation conveniently forgets that the lake had already been in the area for centuries – Shichahai, moreover, is more liable to derive its name from a corruption of 'Tens of Shrines', in recognition of the number of places of worship in the area.

But even as the brutality of the takeover crushed and beat down the last remnants of the old regime, the new Ming dynasty began to build new ministries and public works. One exception was the Mongol-era sewage and drainage system, which was left derelict. For the next few centuries, the removal of night soil was outsourced to carters who would collect it every day, then dry it and sell it as fertiliser on the surrounding fields. As so often happens in Chinese society, human labour was found to be a cheaper and more efficient means of dealing with a problem than modern technology, not least because one man's waste was another man's commodity. This, however, was also the beginning of Ming- and Qing-era Beijing's reputation for smelling awful.

The Centre of the World

Shielding all but the tallest buildings or hilltops from the outside world, the Ming-era city walls remained a defining part of the image of Beijing right up until the time they were demolished in the twentieth century. As late as 1922, the former US ambassador Paul Reinsch could write:

The towers and city walls of Peking, an impressive and astounding apparition of strength and permanence, befit this scene. Solemn and mysterious, memorable for their size, extent and general inevitableness of structure, they can be compared only with the Pyramids, or with great mountains fashioned by the hand of Nature herself.

Down on what was once the south-east corner of the city wall, the shiny glass towers of the Central Business District loom above carefully tended grass verges. The area has the icy, corporate elegance of business districts in American cities – the roads are wide, the sidewalks empty but for street sweepers, the lush grasses well tended but only for show – regular lawn grass does not flourish in parched North China, and is usually replaced with a tough, sharp-bladed facsimile. One could almost believe one were in Atlanta, were it not for the great stone building that sits at the corner of two main roads like a medieval castle, its thick walls crenellated to protect archers from attack, its roof dotted with the distinctive silhouettes of astronomical instruments – a giant metal sextant, a quadrant, an altazi-muth and an armillary sphere.

The Imperial Observatory was originally set up by Khubilai Khan at a different address, but was moved to its current location at the beginning of the Ming dynasty, during one of the city's greatest periods of renovation. It looks like a fortress because that's what it was – it is one of the last remaining pieces of the old city wall, left intact because of its additional function, while other sections were pulled down and moved further out as part of the city's expansion. Victor Meignan wrote in 1885:

> The scientific instruments to be seen there are
> admirable. They are made of bronze, supported on
> feet of the same metal, in which all the fancies of
> Chinese art have been lavished. The contortions of
> these mountings, composed of dragons and grotesque
> monsters, produce a striking contrast to the regular
> forms of the spheres, the parallel lines and astronomical
> figures which they sustain at great height in the air.

Many locals don't know what the building is. Modern slang has truncated its name until it is often dismissed as the 'old observation tower'. One can occasionally find Beijing trainspotters on its battlements, peering down at the approach to the nearby railway station. It seems that for many taxi drivers and passers-by, it is these anoraked figures that are the 'observers'.

The historical truth is even more surprising. The Imperial Observatory was a vital part of the Chinese world order. The superstitions of court religion demanded meticulous calculations for planning auspicious events. The portents had to be precisely right for the dating of a coronation or a royal wedding; government appointments needed to be timed to gain the maximum good fortune. Important decisions and journeys had to be postponed until the exact time when the fates would give them the greatest chance for success. In order to keep tabs on these many factors in the Chinese calendar, the Imperial Observatory was responsible for the planning of almanacs and astronomical tables. At first, the imperial astronomers were locals; then, in the time of Khubilai Khan, many were Muslims.

During the later Ming dynasty, the observatory became the site of quarrelling foreign factions, as the Chinese and Arab astronomers fought to discredit new arrivals from Europe. The Jesuits, of course, hoped to convert the Chinese to Christianity, but planned on playing a long game by first making themselves and their scientific knowledge indispensable. The Jesuits had more accurate equipment than their counterparts, and soon ruled the roost when it came to organising the calendar.

Since the earliest times, when unrest in the Land of Swallows was tracked through the appearances of meteors and comets in the corresponding sector of the sky, the Chinese had believed that the constellations reflect and influence earthly events. But if Beijing were the centre of All Under Heaven, and Beijing's ruler its paramount being, then the rules of propriety demanded that Beijing's centre had a constellation of its own – a central citadel that represented the very axis about which the universe would turn.

Confucius said, 'Ruling by moral example will make you like the pole star, which remains firm in place while the other stars revolve around it.' If Heaven were a map of Earth, then the centre of the world would need to be an earthly analogue of the pole star itself, which was popularly believed by Chinese stargazers to have a purple tint. For this reason, the private citadel at the centre of Beijing, prohibited to commoners for centuries, was known as the 'Purple Forbidden City'. The universe, it was expected, would turn around it, in harmony and awe.

The best time to visit the Forbidden City is off-season, in the dead of winter, when flurries of snow have chased away the tour groups. On a spring day, the early morning crowds are out in force, whisking briskly around the Centre of the Universe in a couple of hours, so the one- and two-day parties can be hurtling down the road in a bus to see the Great Wall before the evening's duck dinner.

The halls tower above the visitor, on stepped ziggurats of marble and alabaster. Draconic gargoyles spit water into the gutters, and great bronze cauldrons sit before each palace – leftovers from the days when the buildings were mostly wooden, and the eunuchs needed a ready source to extinguish localised fires. The tiles beneath my feet are worn down like the flagstones of the Marco Polo Bridge, but not from centuries of attrition. This damage has been done in mere decades, by millions of tramping feet, as armies of tourists roam the main thoroughfares that were once the sole domain of the imperial household. The flagstones are regularly replaced, as are the palaces themselves, renovated in permanent rotation. Some have glassed facades, permitting views of shadowy interiors stacked with dusty memorabilia of the imperial era. Others have been fitted with turnstile gates, hoping to relieve the visitor of a few more coins for that little bit extra – an exhibition of royal jewellery, perhaps, or some objets d'art from a particular reign.

In the shadow of the great halls there are smaller buildings, used in the past by government officers. Here, there is a building where the military had their quartermaster. Here is another where young princes received their schooling.

The approach to the Hall of Preserving Harmony, as in many other imperial buildings, features twin staircases, separated by a carved alabaster image of dragons twirling through clouds. The strange design is a stirring relic of the imperial era – the space between the staircases is decorated because it would never be walked upon. Instead, the emperor was borne up the stairs in his litter. He would float above the dragon images in his chair, while his litter-bearers trudged up the steps either side. In the northern sector are the private apartments of the imperial family, surrounded by carefully landscaped gardens, scattered with pavilions and teahouses. These days, there is also a display of numerous funny-shaped rocks, presented to the emperor as birthday presents. He would probably have preferred socks.

These days, it is known locally as the 'old palace' (*Gu Gong*). It is a mandatory inclusion for the tourist, somewhat to its detriment, since its sheer size and the weight of its story can over-awe the unprepared visitor. For many foreigners, the Forbidden City soon leads to the common condition of feeling 'templed out'. Its side passages are a maze of anonymous russet walls, its gardens an identikit of intricate but nameless buildings. The greatest service done for the site was by Bernardo Bertolucci, whose 1987 movie *The Last Emperor* helped untold millions of foreigners to appreciate the Forbidden City in context.

But this is the place where *The Last Emperor* happened. Not merely the location for the Bertolucci film, but the actual place where 'Henry' Puyi, final Lord of Ten Thousand Years, once frightened the eunuchs by riding on a bicycle. Within the complex, by the ubiquitous postcard sellers, behind the cash machine, is the place where a terrifying Manchu general turned on the steps to address a crowd, announcing that he would be taking over, against the background of a smouldering palace building.

The Forbidden City was the centrepiece of Ming- and Qing-era Beijing. Much of what remains today is more recent, from the Ming's Qing usurpers, but even so, the basic design has been retained, a recreation of the ancient idea of the centre of the perfect city, at the centre of the perfect world, presided over by the perfect ruler.

Beyond the walls of the Forbidden City, Ming-era Beijing struggled to live up to the architectural plan. Rivers and lakes unhelpfully broke up some of the straight-line streets. The expansion of the outer walls of the city north, creating a suburb that would have completely surrounded the Forbidden City, was never completed, forcing the idealised urban design to fall a little short of the Yongle Emperor's ambitions.

The family of dragons, that old favourite, was soon back in local myth, sneaking into town in human form to suck wells dry. The family was defeated at last by the architect Liu Bowen, who successfully arranged for the diversion of waters from a nearby river. One legend tells of a stonemason working on the Beijing project, who thought he saw the dragons making off with the water and gave chase, only to be lured into a dry riverbed just before the floodgates were opened, bringing a fatal torrent crashing down upon him. To hear the story told, it seems suspiciously close to an old tale of a sacrifice to a river god.

But Beijing's water supply remains salty and faintly unpleasant – said to be the last revenge of the dragons, who hoard all the good water at the Jade Spring in the hills and leave Beijing with nothing but the dregs. The residents of the imperial citadel thwarted the dragons with a daily convoy of carts that rolled into the hills and to the Jade Spring, where they stocked up with fresh water and brought it back to the palace. In the evenings, they would be replaced by sewage-bearing 'honey wagons', heading out of the city with a very different cargo. Occasionally, exploratory wells would happen upon better supplies inside the city, and wealthy locals would soon buy up the daily supply, such as in Wangfujing ('well of the prince'). Geomancers attempted to read some sort of pattern into the occasional discoveries, claiming that the sites of good wells in

Ming-dynasty Beijing followed the shape of a giant centipede sent to burrow into the earth by a sorcerer who was tired of the bitter taste of Beijing tea.

The unnamed wizard was not the only supernatural assistant. A story about the strangely ornate watchtowers of the Forbidden City claims that Yongle ordered his masons to come up with something distinctive on pain of death and then left them to it. After three months of deliberation (notably, the same deadline given to Khubilai's bell-makers in Mongol times), the builders were running out of patience and hope, and one of the carpenters went outside to get some air. There, he bumped into an aged pedlar who sold him an elaborate cricket cage. Back in the meeting room, the carpenter showed it to his fellow workers, who marvelled at the construction that somehow used nine beams and eighteen pillars to create a roof with seventy-two ridges. The builders copied the cricket cage for the construction of the watchtowers. Later folklore suggested that the cricket seller had really been the God of Carpenters in disguise.

But much of the folklore about the Forbidden City relates to its outer courts – those parts, such as the watchtowers, that could be glimpsed by commoners. There is a fascination for the historian in being able to stand in the places that centuries of people could only read about in dynastic chronicles – the inner chambers where empresses watched acrobats, or the well where a concubine was murdered or took her own life (depending on whom one believes). The Forbidden City is a place to be savoured over many visits, coupled with reading and appreciation of the many historical moments it has witnessed. The half-day allotted to so many tour groups seems like a pointless exercise – a perplexing parade of names and dates, delivered amid big open spaces, and occasional glimpses into dark rooms. One first visits the Forbidden City out of a sense of duty. Its true majesty and wondrous history takes a lifetime to appreciate.

Although he is remembered as the architect of Ming Beijing, Yongle did not flourish in his new capital. The paint was barely dry on the new Forbidden City when it became the home to scandal. Beijing might have represented a new start for the Ming dynasty, but despite being far removed from the old capitals in the South, it spontaneously developed troubles of its own.

Southern Chinese beauties, those capricious, wilful creatures that had brought down many an emperor in past centuries, were in short supply in Beijing. But that did not seem to bother Yongle – in fact, his particular fetish seems to have been for foreign girls, particularly Koreans from just over the border. One such concubine, Lady Quan, died soon after Yongle's return from a campaign, and was later found to have been poisoned by a rival, who had arranged for arsenic to be dropped into the poor girl's tea. The matter only came to light several years later as part of palace feud between two other Koreans, when a girl from a poor background accused a snooty palace rival of being the poisoner.

The alleged poisoner was branded, and she is said to have died 'soon afterwards' – an indicator of suicide, whether enforced or voluntary. The accuser fared little better, since she later hanged herself, afraid that her platonic relationship with a palace eunuch might be regarded as a betrayal of her imperial master. Yongle, however, refused to believe this explanation, and tortured the dead lady's servants until they 'confessed' that she had killed herself because she was afraid the emperor would discover she was planning to assassinate him.

The allegation led to a savage purge of palace women, with over two thousand eventually implicated and tortured to death. The real truth came out in the dying curse of one of the victims, who alleged that Yongle was impotent. Beijing life had given him terrible rheumatism and left him unable to carry out his conjugal duties. This had left his many dozens of concubines and wives with perilously little to do and had turned them all upon each other.

The Eight Great Sights
With such bad omens, it is perhaps no surprise that the Chinese began to suspect that their almanacs might be in error. Yongle's successors kept careful tabs on matters of state feng shui, questioning many of his city-planning decisions. The temple complex to Heaven and Earth he had built in the southern suburbs was radically remodelled. One of its most distinctive buildings, the multi-eaved circular Hall of Prayer for Good Harvests (today simply called the Temple of Heaven) has become one of the most recognisable buildings in Beijing, although the version that exists today is relatively recent. The Ming-dynasty original was struck by lightning and burned to the ground in 1889, although the modern building is supposedly a reasonable facsimile. Not that Victor Meignan's account of it in 1885 is liable to lead to a flood of visitors:

I shall say little of the Temple of Heaven and the Temple of Agriculture, because they are not interesting. The first especially is unworthy of the exalted name it bears. It is an immense park surrounded with walls, in which chapels and pretty pavilions, covered with blue porcelain, are distributed, and where a subdued light penetrates through blinds composed of little tubes of blue glass placed parallel. A platform of white marble is raised in the middle of the park, and it is here the Emperor occasionally comes to offer with his own hand sacrifices to the Divinity.

After 1534, when Earth-worship was moved to a new, more geomantically appropriate location, the complex was given over entirely to the worship of Heaven, and it still has its remarkable circular multi-tiered altar. For many centuries, this was the location of one of the most important ceremonies of the imperial calendar. On the day before the Winter Solstice, the emperors of the Ming and Qing dynasties would leave the Forbidden City in a great procession that nobody would see – the people of Beijing were ordered to remain indoors on pain of death, while the religious procession marched on a road strewn with yellow dust towards the great Altar of Heaven. The ceremony began before dawn, involving parties of carefully coordinated 'temple dancers' on the lower tiers of the site. The emperor himself, however, was left alone at the pinnacle of the altar, standing before symbolic offerings to the spirits and his ancestors, while a herald read out his prayers, his respects and an annual report of events and accomplishments in the empire. The ceremony would finish with the ceremonial burning of sacrificial offerings, in a series of braziers that flanked the altar, each leading to a great tiled sacrificial oven.

Yongle's workers also radically rebuilt the Mongol walls, which seem to have been largely comprised of rammed earth and were subject to decay and erosion if left untended. The Ming builders faced the earthen ramparts with bricks or, in some cases, built completely new walls within the perimeter of the old ones – the depopulation of the plague period left the former khan's city not requiring anything near the land area of its heyday.

Wall-building also went on outside the city, to legendary effect. The most visible achievement of Yongle's dynasty, begun in his lifetime but not completed until decades later, was the most famous monument of all in China: the Great Wall. The Ming wall was not the first to mark out the northern border of China, but it was a much more enduring undertaking than its predecessors. Whereas previous 'great walls', dating back to the time of the Qin dynasty and the First Emperor, had utilised rammed earth, wooden palisades and ditches, the Ming wall was a sturdy bricks-and-mortar affair. Earlier walls had often been used less as border markers and more as bases from which Chinese troops and colonists could sally forth against the enemies of the North and West. Yongle's wall had a genuine defensive role, with construction commencing in recognition of a new policy towards the Mongols. Unable to hound China's former rulers to a final defeat in their homeland, the Ming dynasty instead hoped to wall them off, putting them out of sight and mind.

Despite Yongle's successors defining the northern border of China with iconic finality, there were soon Chinese colonists to the north of it. Ironically, it was those colonists' relationship with the Manchu people to the north that encouraged the Manchus to consider ruling China for themselves. When the Ming dynasty eventually fell, Chinese colonists from north of the wall, who had gone just native enough to serve new masters, would fill many critical roles in the invading forces.

Today, much of the wall remains in ruins, although several portions have been painstakingly restored to their Ming-era glory. US president Richard Nixon became one of the first high-profile foreign visitors to a restored section, apocryphally reported to have proclaimed, 'It sure is a great wall.' In the decades that have followed, the Great Wall has become an industry of its own, and the Badaling section that Nixon saw has become something of a tourist trap. It is close enough to Beijing that a tour bus can take in both Badaling and the Ming Tombs in one day, meaning that, although the wall is supposedly thousands of miles long, its sections nearest Beijing are crawling with people.

Recent years have seen other sections restored, with decisions based largely on either transport access or the opportunity offered for an impressive backdrop. Broken-down sections first attract tourists off the beaten track, then the inevitable hawkers, then the renovators and safety consultants, who often strip away much of the historical charm along with the dangers. Today, one must drive for several hours to find a relatively deserted section of the Great Wall, and visitors are discouraged from doing so – far better, for all concerned, that they are corralled into an area with handrails, public transport access and a restaurant.

Standing on the Great Wall is a beautiful and terrifying experience. It still has the same effect on modern visitors that it was designed to have on the Mongols. Stretching away as far as the eye can see across mountains and valleys until it peters out on the horizon, only to lurch back into view again as it rings a strategic site a few miles further over, the Great Wall still sends a message to any who see it. *This is what China can do*, it says. *Not just to you, but to ourselves* – not for nothing did earlier defensive projects gain the wall the nickname of 'the longest cemetery'. The Great Wall is a testament to the millions that died to build it and a symbol of fortress China.

Yongle also laid the earliest foundations of Beijing's tourist industry by commanding his ministers to come up with a list of peerless attractions that could be promoted as the Eight Great Sights of Beijing. His reasoning was political, aimed not at encouraging vacationing visitors but at whipping up a sense of local heritage. Yongle still faced unsteady support in the South, and his Eight Great Sights project was designed to encourage poems, songs and prose to establish Beijing's image as a true capital – and hence his own as the rightful ruler. These eight wonders of Beijing, as chronicled in the early Ming dynasty, are a dreary collection of half-hearted seasonal slogans, sounding precisely like the kind of nonsense one might get in a new town without many old or famous landmarks, from a committee who could not be bothered to look too far from their office window.

The Marco Polo Bridge, still standing after many centuries, was dragged in as one of the exhibits, notably because it had cropped up in a poem from one of the emperors of the Jin dynasty. What was good enough for the Khitans was good enough for the Ming: the moon at dawn on the Marco Polo Bridge. The Great Wall was also a mandatory inclusion, although the feature chosen was not technically part of the wall proper, but an isolated fortress on a mountain pass, tarted up with an irrelevant spot of nature promotion to become one of the Eight Great Sights: the lush greenery around the fortress at Juyong Pass. The committee followed up with the sun on the Golden Terrace (a site that is no longer extant). Seeing a pattern that might do their selection for them, they scrabbled around for more natural elements and opposites. The trees around the old ruined entrance to the ancient capital, the Thistle Gate – they might do. But, since there was already a mention of greenery, the committee added that the sight was only 'great' when the forest was viewed in the mist. There were pretty rainbows out in the hills, in the mists where the Jade Spring of fresh water bubbled to the surface... so they heard. Snow looked good on the Western Hills... sometimes. In spring, it was often pleasantly warm on Hortensia Island... apparently. The ripples on the water, the committee decided, looked nice in Beihai Park. And that was the eight done – conspicuously with a couple being visible from the same spot, as if someone had dashed off the last two as an afterthought on his way to work.

Even more lost to prosperity are the sounds of old Beijing. One still gets an occasional echo in the calls of street hawkers, but the noise and bustle of the streets, the clapping boards of storytellers summoning a crowd, the gongs and firecrackers of a wedding procession, the thud and clatter of carts, have all been crowded out by new technologies and new machineries. Perhaps the most iconic sound of the old city was that of the Drum Tower and Bell Tower, once the sites of the city's daily and nightly time-keeping but now silent fortresses in the north of the city.

The drums were struck quickly for eighteen beats and then slowly for eighteen in three rounds, for a total of 108 beats, signifying not only that all was well but that it was time to shut down the streets for curfew. The drum would then be struck every two hours to mark time through the night. One guide for scholars suggested a quick round of shadow-boxing in the courtyard at the sounding of the midnight drum in order to enliven the senses for further study. The author Xu Chengbei managed in 2001 to find an elderly man who remembered the sound from his childhood, associating it with the end of playtime:

> I could hear the sound of the drum and bell every evening ... The sound was agreeable yet awe-inspiring. I often heard such words: 'Stop messing about now. It's time to go to bed. Don't you hear the drum?' I rarely heard the midnight drum. When I heard it I was rather scared. I don't know why.

The bell would be rung (108 times) at 5 a.m. and 7 p.m. It was last used to mark time in 1924, when its chime was said to be audible for up to 20 kilometres. A modern experiment found it to be almost entirely muffled within a few blocks by the ambient clamour of modern Beijing.

The Advent of the Manchus

The desire to keep Beijing as the capital, and to maintain relations with the peoples even further north, risked recreating the old North–South divide. Far to the south, Nanjing was kept as a sleepy alternate capital, its ministers and officials diligently shadowing the functions of the true centre, just in case Beijing should have to be abandoned. Even as the campaigns against the Mongols petered out, and the Ming mindset became more about hiding behind walls than proactively pursuing new frontiers, the Ming people continued to intermix across the border.

Nanjing, as it would eventually turn out, was not the only place that was shadowing Beijing. North of the Great Wall, the people of Manchuria were developing a love, respect and covetousness towards the power and wealth of the Ming dynasty. In their own capital of Mukden (modern Shenyang), the Manchus began to formulate ministries and offices designed to copy and eventually surpass those of the Chinese in Beijing. Eventually, the ruling clan of the Manchus proclaimed a new decree – that the Ming dynasty was fated to fall, and that it was the destiny of the Manchus to replace it. Just as Khubilai Khan had proclaimed the foundation of his Yuan dynasty several years before conquering China, the Manchus proclaimed their own replacement for the Ming somewhat in advance of their actual rule. At first, they called it the Jin ('golden') dynasty in imitation of their Jurchen cousins of old.

In China, the Ming dynasty staggered and stumbled, barely able to pay the troops who staffed the Great Wall. Bad weather led to bad harvests, in turn creating famine and disease. The Ming general Wu Sangui, charged with holding back the northern barbarians, held his army together with charisma and promises, until the fateful day when he switched sides.

Dwindling finances on the wall were not the only sign of trouble. Rebellions in the hinterland offered still more worries to the fretful Ming dynasty. Even as thousands of Ming soldiers stared northwards from the battlements of the Great Wall, Beijing fell to a Chinese rebel. Li Zicheng, a former postman, had led a bandit existence for several years before leading his forces to the gates of Beijing itself. The city fell swiftly, its troops demoralised, its cannons without ammunition, it defences compromised by years of neglect and corruption.

At the Great Wall, the Ming general Wu chose a new and deadly alliance, inviting the Manchus to accompany him in a mission to relieve the capital. They never left.

A great battle in a sandstorm was fought at Shahe ('sandy river'), now a station on the Changping subway line. Travel by car or bus to Badaling to see the Great Wall and you are sure to pass it, marked by a huge statue of Li Zicheng on horseback at the off-ramp for the Ming Tombs. The People's Republic of China chooses to commemorate him, the commoner who overthrew an empire for a scant few weeks, rather than the Ming general who made a fateful Faustian pact to destroy him.

Usually known in Chinese simply as the 'thirteen tombs'

(Shisan Ling), the Ming Tombs – a final resting place for all the emperors of the Ming dynasty from Yongle's time to its end – were once a day's ride outside the city. Today the site is a stop on the Changping line that branches from Xi'er Qi (Line 12), about an hour from the centre of town. The necropolis stretches for miles along the foothills of the mountains but, while it is rewarding for hikers to wander among the many pavilions and tumbledown monuments, only a handful of the sites are technically tourist-friendly.

Although every tomb has a 'sacred way' approach road, the first, largest and best is the tomb of Yongle, the Emperor of Perpetual Happiness. The tomb itself is not open, but the courtyards and pavilions of the temple buildings make for a pleasant, if dusty, museum of Yongle's life. Also open to the public is Zhaoling, the tomb of Wanli's father, Longqing (1537–72), the Emperor of Grand Celebration, which is the most complete and undamaged mausoleum extant at the site. A hiker can spend a happy day wandering the ruins of the other sites at the necropolis. If I had to pick a favourite, it would be the one that is actually on the other side of the river, off to the west of the main Sacred Way. It is far less impressive on the outside than others, because it was never intended to hold the body of an emperor. Siling was originally built to hold the body of a favourite concubine of Chongzhen, the Emperor of Lofty Omens (1611–44). This was that same unfortunate Ming ruler who presided over the country's multiple crises of crop failures, famine and foreign invasion, and who hanged himself, aged thirty-three, at the foot of Coal Hill as the soldiers of Li Zicheng marched into town. After his death, he was hastily interred in this humble spot. Touchingly close by is a memorial tablet to Wang Cheng'en, his most loyal eunuch, who followed his master in suicide. Siling makes for a melancholy coda to the majesty of the Ming dynasty; in comparison to the palatial tomb of Yongle nearby, it is little more than a pauper's grave.

As for the Manchu hordes who accompanied Wu through the wall and into Beijing, their monuments are all around you.

5

'Peking': 1644–1912

For a moment, I am alone in the chamber. The walls are painted in the bright red of marital bliss. The screen in front of me is adorned with a giant pattern comprising double *xi* ('happiness'), a traditional nuptial decoration. This quiet, deserted hall looks much like any other to the average Western visitor, particularly on a day trip to the Forbidden City, where one large bare room in a big red hall can often end up looking very much like another. But there is something special about this place, with its double happiness on the wall and entwined dragon and phoenix designs repeated on the furniture. The lanterns similarly bear a double *xi* design. This quiet hall, this very room, is a place of bridal celebration. Three different Qing emperors spent their wedding nights here. They drank wine with their new brides on this very bed. There is joy in this room, but also nervousness and pathos. Of the three emperors, two of them died young in suspicious circumstances, the victims of palace conspiracies by old widows determined to cling to power. The silence is remarkable, as is the chill – even though it is a warm, sunny day outside, I see a cloud of my breath in the air.

The haunting silence is broken by an ear-splitting mechanical shriek – a handheld loudhailer that has a built-in tune. At the touch of a button, it blares the first few bars of the *Laurel and Hardy* theme at a decibel level twice that of the average ice cream van. It is in the hands of an earnest Chinese guide, who has used it to shock a group of Italian tourists into stunned silence.

'This is the hall of earthly tranquillity!' she yells into her megaphone. 'Former residence of the empresses and a place of silent contemplation!'

A Square atop a Rectangle

Although history books usually show a tidy single date for the regime change, the fall of Beijing to the Manchus in 1644 did not bring the rest of China immediately with it. A resistance movement continued for another generation, until the last rebels either forgot what they were fighting for or faded into organisations indistinguishable from criminal gangs. In an unguarded moment at a banquet, one Manchu nobleman claimed that his people originally had little expectation of taking China south of the Yellow River. Instead, they had set their sights on seizing the northern territory once held by the Khitans and Jurchen, but had been startled by the lack of true Ming resistance and by the numbers of Chinese subjects willing to join their cause. As a result, in the early days of the Qing dynasty, the Manchus did not have much time for rebuilding. The surviving structures of the old Ming Forbidden City were simply repurposed for the new owners, with little more than a change in signposts and the occasional lick of paint. It took many years before Qing-era buildings began to replace those of the departed dynasty in the centre of Beijing.

Qing-era Beijing long retained a sense of being an occupied territory. It was divided into two walled cities, a square atop a rectangle. The 'Manchu' city, the walls of which are now traced by the path of Line 2 of the subway, was home to the conquerors. A smaller 'Chinese' city stretched several city blocks from what is now the bottom corner of Tiananmen Square to what is now the southern edge of the Second Ring Road – this, too, follows the outline of the old city. Little trace of its towering, crenelated walls survives today, except for the vestigial names of long-gone gates and a small stretch left standing in the south-east corner of the Manchu town.

The fall of the Ming dynasty created a number of villains for Chinese history, on every side of the conflict. The last Ming emperors were painted as unworthy successors to the noble Chinese who had ousted the Mongols, having failed their subjects and their ancestors by losing the support of Heaven once more. Wu Sangui is a classically tragic figure in Chinese drama – a soldier torn between his allegiance to a doomed dynasty, temptations on offer from devilish invaders and a desire for revenge against the usurper who killed his father and raped his lover. Only Li Zicheng has gained some form of rehabilitation. In the Communist era, he was lionised for his role in toppling the old imperial order and for attracting humble farmers to his standard, eventually becoming the subject of an influential 1963 historical novel by Yao Xueyin (sadly not yet translated).

The Manchus ruled China during a tumultuous period in which geography no longer kept it out of contact with other powers. Ironically, Beijing was more isolated than China's peripheries, with the capital being walled in by desert and mountains to the north and its closest sea port, in Tianjin, being iced up from November to March every year. During the Age of Exploration, as the Portuguese and Spanish rounded Africa and mapped the Americas, the Chinese stayed put. In the earliest days of the Ming dynasty, Chinese embassies had sailed as far as Madagascar, but the great age of Chinese exploration was soon at an end. Finances dwindled, and the Ming emperors had other problems on their minds. Besides, it was thought unseemly that imperial embassies would go in search of recognition of their own greatness from foreigners – far better that the barbarians approach China themselves, with the correct degree of etiquette and a fair amount of fear and trembling. Beijing itself may have played some part in this: the landlocked capital, forever clinging to its inland canals and its camel trains across the plains, may have encouraged a landlubber attitude in its ruling class. While southern people – in the great river port of Nanjing or the seafaring towns of Fuzhou and Guangzhou – had long traditions of maritime trade, northerners preferred to look inwards, at the great sea of grassland that extended to the west or the parched, dusty deserts of the hinterland.

The Manchus were even more landlocked than the Ming dynasty. With a nomadic background and a love of horsemanship and the steppe life, the Manchu ruling house was pathologically afraid of the sea. In the seventeenth century, it briefly ordered the complete depopulation of the sea coast to a distance of some 50 kilometres, hoping to cut China off completely from the undue influence of the coastline. Instead of building a navy, the Manchus briefly attempted to push the sea itself out of mind, creating a swathe of barren territory more than a day's march across, patrolled only by government troops with orders to kill any loiterers on sight. With such an attitude, it is perhaps not surprising that the arrival of the European nations in the Far East took the Manchus by surprise.

Beijing's northern location played a part in China's decline during the eighteenth and nineteenth centuries. Contact with European powers was initially limited to the far South of the Chinese continent, through the port of Canton. Europeans pushed for further trading opportunities and contacts inland, but Beijing remained largely unimpressed by their requests and entreaties and unaware of their urgency. Arguably, the protocols and politesse of Chinese government communiqués, in continuing to bow and scrape before the emperor's majesty, misled him as to the seriousness of the situation.

The aging British ambassador George Macartney (later Lord Macartney) arrived in China in 1793, hoping to establish diplomatic relations. Instead, he scandalised the Manchu court by refusing to kowtow before the Qianlong Emperor and by looking down his nose at a valuable gift of jade. Meanwhile, the emperor was baffled by Macartney's entreaties; China was the centre of the world and prided itself on needing nothing from barbarian neighbours. The concept of 'trade' was entirely beyond the emperor, who advised Macartney, 'You ... should simply act in conformity with our wishes by strengthening your loyalty and swearing perpetual obedience, so as to ensure that your country may share the blessings of peace.'

Lanes and Alleys

Macartney left a record of the days that he spent in Beijing that October, writing that the city was 'one of the largest in the world, and justly to be admired for its walls and gates, the distribution of its quarters, the width and allineation of its streets, the grandeur of its triumphal arches and the number and magnificence of its palaces'. The city that Macartney saw still bore reminders that the Manchus were conquerors – policing was 'singularly strict', and Macartney was surprised by a curfew that effectively closed down every main street, 'shut up by barricades at each end and a guard ... constantly patrolling'. He was also taken aback by the population's close-packed living arrangements:

> At Pekin one scarcely meets with any but men, as the women seldom stir abroad. The houses ... are very closely inhabited, it being no uncommon thing for a dozen people to be crowded into one small chamber that in England would be considered as a scanty accommodation for a single person ... None of the streets are paved so that in wet weather they are covered in mud and in dry weather the dust is excessively disagreeable pervading every place and every thing, but what renders it intolerably offensive is the stench.

The city retained a 'chessboard' design of wide thoroughfares, as mentioned by Marco Polo, and within each square was a maze of small alleys and tracks. Strictly speaking, a street that runs east–west is called a *hutong* ('alley') while one that runs north–south is called a *xiang* ('lane'). The terms were in use since the Han dynasty but came to be associated with the Manchu period, not least because the Manchu word for a well, *huttog*, sounded similar, and led many historians to assume in error that such architecture began with the Manchu conquest. The terms remained an integral part of Beijing life well into the twentieth century, as recalled by Ellen LaMotte in 1916:

> You wind your way along a narrow, unpaved street, or *hutong* – a street full of little open-air shops, cook-shops, stalls of various kinds, and then come upon a high, blank wall with a pair of stone lions at the gateway and an enormous red lacquer gate, heavily barred, and that's your house. The gateman opens to your ring, and as the big doors swing back, you see nothing of the courtyard ... you are confronted by the devil screen, a high stone wall [that] ... blocks the evil spirits that fly in when the compound gates are opened – the blind evil spirits, that can only fly in straight paths, and hence crash against the devil screen when they enter.

In fact, the hutong represents the most traditional form of Chinese architecture imaginable, comprising multiple clusters of *siheyuan* ('quadrangles') – small courtyards with long, low houses running all around their walls, but for the opening afforded by a central gate. The main reason that women 'seldom stirred abroad' in Macartney's observation was that courtyard life served to keep them mainly occupied, safe behind their four walls but still with ample room to work and socialise.

The names of the hutongs retain glimpses of a lost Beijing, including more than six hundred named for nearby temples; two hundred containing the word *ying*, for camps in what were once open fields; 132 with *qiao*, in recognition of nearby bridges; and some sixty-two named *cang* or *kui*, for the presence of nearby grain silos or storehouses. Others have fantastically evocative names that bring history to life. Fenzhang Hutong means 'creating music diligently', although that was the result of some careful lobbying by a musician who bought land in the area in the early twentieth century and didn't much like its original name, Fenchang Hutong. That name literally meant 'turd factory', harking back to its days as a station processing night soil into fertiliser. Baofeng Hutong is named after the leopard kennels where the Ming emperors kept their big cats. Some have more modern name changes for euphony or to reflect political trends, such as Babaolou ('eight treasure houses') Hutong, which suddenly became Miezi ('end capitalism') Hutong in the 1960s. (It's Babaolou again today, capitalism having inconveniently not ended.)

Originally, many of these cloister-like dwellings were mansions for the well-off. The hutongs in the 'Chinese' city were simpler dwellings. But the 'Manchu' city amounted to a human shield around the Forbidden City, with the entire area subdivided into eight districts, one for each of the Manchu legions – four with plain colours, and four with fringed banners. The Wangfujing area, for example, was once home to the families of the Bordered White Banner. The Yonghegong area, around the Lama Temple to the north, was the area of the Bordered Yellow Banner; the

Drum Tower and Bell Tower marked the border between that and the district of the Plain Yellow Banner.

In the days after the Manchu conquest, these were privileged locations but, as the Qing dynasty stagnated, many devolved into slums, particularly in the period after 1911, when the bannermen of the Manchu city lost their imperial stipend. As time passed, particularly in the impecunious later Qing era, or the egalitarian Communist era, many of the old *siheyuan* buildings were subdivided, so that four or more families would have rooms in the same structure. As modernity slowly took hold, the shared wells for clusters of hutongs transformed into standpipes, and ultimately into communal toilets and washrooms.

Foreign Mud

Macartney was not wrong about the dust. Beijing was frozen solid in winter, baked dry in summer and subject to horrific dust storms at other times. Ellen LaMotte described the latter:

> These dust-storms are the curse of Peking, and of north China ... It blows in straight from the Gobi desert and makes the late winter and the spring, particularly the spring, almost intolerable. Since our return we have been having dust-storms on an average of twice a week, big ones and little ones, lasting from a few hours to several days. There are two kinds: surface storms, when a tremendous wind blows dense clouds of fine sharp dust along the streets ... and overhead storms, which ... are a curious phenomenon: fine, red, powdery dust

is whirled up into the higher levels of the atmosphere blown overhead by the upper air currents, from which it drifts down, covering everything in sight. On such occasions, there is frequently no wind at all on the streets, but the air is so filled with dust that the sun appears as in a fog, a red disk showing dimly through the thick, dense atmosphere.

Like the Mongols, the Manchu emperors did not enjoy Beijing dust, preferring to live some 15 kilometres outside the Forbidden City in a series of mansions and sculpted gardens near the Jade Spring, known collectively outside China as the Summer Palace.

The title is a misnomer. Although officially intended as a residence for the hot months, the Summer Palace proved irresistible for much of the year, its name implying that the sovereigns were hard at work in the capital for longer than they actually were. They often packed up and headed for the Summer Palace as early as the Chinese New Year in February. At the height of summer itself, they often sought even cooler climes many leagues to the north. Kangxi, the Emperor of Hearty Prosperity, spent as much time at the Summer Palace as his court responsibilities would allow. His son and successor, Yongzheng, the Emperor of Harmonious Justice, effectively moved his administration to the gardens and built extra palaces in its southern quarter so he could run the state without leaving them. By the time of Yongzheng's successor, Qianlong, the Emperor of Strong Prosperity, the Summer Palace was arguably more important to the imperial family than the Forbidden City itself.

The Summer Palace's finest garden was later known as the Yuanming Yuan ('garden of perfect brightness'), the 'Versailles of the Orient', with a large lake, around which were clustered nine connected islets, each representing one of the ancient ducal domains. Its beauty was legendary, although not everybody was impressed; George Macartney, on the British mission of 1793, found it to contain a 'singularity of Chinese taste which ... in truth is by no means worthy of our copying'. To Macartney's mind, 'the impropriety is glaring and argues sickly and declining taste, meant solely to display vanity and expense'.

But for almost everybody else it was a triumph of what is now called hybridity, as the Chinese emperors fell in love with the exotic imagery and trinkets of the distant West, with which they were plied by their Jesuit confidantes. Meanwhile, in the West, Europe fell in love with chinoiserie, as Jesuit accounts of the pomp and grandeur of China created a fad for porcelain, follies and 'oriental' decoration. With bitter historical irony, the West would advance on the East for the next century, and the Summer Palace would pay the price.

Other landscaped gardens were clustered nearby, including the Yihe Yuan ('garden of nurtured harmony'), set around a former reservoir for old Beijing's water supply, now remodelled as Kunming Lake, a whimsical recreation of idyllic southern living. Fairy-tale pagodas, statues and pavilions were dotted around the lake and in the hills above, creating a false-perspective impression of being deep in the countryside, far away from the bustle of the capital.

A bronze ox, its back carved with a sacred spell to

suppress floodwaters, gazes out over the lake, close to the majestic Seventeen Arch Bridge that reaches out to an island in the centre of the lake. The ox's presence suggests climatic troubles elsewhere – floods had heavily damaged the Marco Polo Bridge downriver in 1698, and its modern-day collection of stone lions mixes thousand-year-old originals with more recent carvings in the old style. Kangxi, the Emperor of Hearty Prosperity, also renamed the waterway itself, changing it from the Wuding ('capricious') River to the Yongding ('eternally pacified') River, hoping thereby to make it behave.

Floods, droughts and occasional famines were nothing new. But China was entirely unprepared for the arrival of the European powers. Towards the end of the Ming dynasty, European visitors had been treated with amusement and condescension in Beijing. By the 1700s, the European community in Beijing was growing. The Russians were the first sizeable group, as emissaries of the great European power were able to literally walk all the way east to Siberia and then south. As marine technology advanced in great leaps, seafaring nations, particularly the British, were soon following behind. Then, as now, China was recognised as a market with gargantuan potential, ready to be moulded, coerced or even bullied into cooperation.

Lord Macartney's kindly entreaties to the Chinese hid a source of great urgency: the balance of trade between the English, who had a thirst for Chinese tea, and the Chinese, who famously claimed that they wanted for nothing. The American Revolution had cut off old trade routes across the Atlantic, and Napoleon was on the rise in Europe. The

British took extreme measures by finding a new cargo that they could sell to the Chinese in exchange for tea: opium. British popular myth, particularly in the old Chinatown of London's Limehouse district, would later suggest that the Chinese were a race of addled dope fiends. Such stories tended to avoid the inner truth that China's people had been made so by British salesmen. Opium ('foreign mud' to the Chinese) was grown and harvested in India, then shipped to South China, where the British became drug pushers to an entire nation.

The exponential rise in the number of opium addicts in the south was a cause of concern to the Chinese. The government in Beijing tried to ban the sale of opium and imposed severe punishments on smugglers and sellers of the drug. But such well-intentioned decrees were of little use in the South, where forceful British officials such as Charles (Lord) Napier were demanding ever-greater trade privileges. The Chinese administrator Lin Zexu wrote a stern letter to Queen Victoria, demanding that she rein in her pushers, but the message never reached the British monarch, who was herself an occasional dabbler in opium. The frustrated Lin eventually seized and burned all the opium in Canton in a heady conflagration in 1839 – the deed is celebrated in one of the tableaux on the Monument to the People's Heroes in today's Tiananmen Square. His bold act was answered with the arrival of a British fleet brandishing modern cannons that far exceeded anything the Chinese had to offer. In one of several actions later collectively known as the Opium War, a fleet sailed up the Yangtze and effectively cut the Chinese empire in two, blocking Beijing's tax and trade conduits to the South. China was obliged in 1843 to concede to the Treaty of Nanjing, an infamous document that opened certain Chinese ports to British trade and permitted the entry of Christian missionaries into the country.

Chinese schoolbooks still regard this as the beginning of a Century of Humiliation, leading to a series of further incursions and unequal treaties that were not halted until the proclamation of the People's Republic in 1949. Emissaries arrived from other countries, each determined to grab concessions on the Chinese coast ready to trade in the hinterland. Without a strong military or any means of resisting forces bolstered by the Industrial Revolution (which had, until that point, largely passed China by), the Manchus were forced to concede several strategic towns and ports to foreign leases. The two most famous, kept in foreign hands until the very end of the twentieth century, were Hong Kong (UK) and Macao (Portugal), although China is littered with evidence of other concessions, now forgotten. Shanghai, Fuzhou, Guangzhou and Tianjin still have handsome boulevards built for Europeans, while Harbin's architecture alludes to its former status as the 'Moscow of the East', and Qingdao retains a German brewery (Tsing Tao) set up by its European expats.

Equally embarrassing was the imposition of 'extraterritoriality' – the new arrivals treated the Chinese in much the same way as they had already treated the colonised populations of America and Africa. It was decreed that Chinese laws and restrictions did not apply to Europeans – a stinging insult to the world's oldest continuous culture, which was now not even permitted to legally arrest, try or detain foreign criminals on its own territory. The cherry on the cake was the concept of Most Favoured Nation status, wherein any concessions granted to one power would have to also be granted to another.

The imperial household in Beijing was no longer the master of its own country, and it was only a matter of time before this led to open unrest. Simple protests over food shortages or local injustice were often magnified along unwelcome political lines – in particular, much of the unrest in mid- to late-nineteenth-century China dragged up the old spectre of the Ming dynasty, serving to remind the 'Han' Chinese that, even though they were suffering indignities at the hands of foreigners, their own rulers were a clan from what was then regarded as outside China proper. As Manchu power weakened, whispers that they had lost the support of Heaven began, and became all the louder after 1853, when the Yellow River dramatically and disastrously shifted its course so that it flowed to the south, not the north, of the Shandong peninsula, devastating thousands of square kilometres of farmland.

Religious and criminal movements suggested that it was time for a change. Ethnic minorities in isolated areas proclaimed rebellious enclaves that often went unpunished for years, while criminal elements took advantage of bad feeling towards the Manchus to paint their unlawful activities with a brush of Ming restorationism, or even the establishment of a completely new order.

In the South, the first sign was the cataclysmic Taiping Rebellion – more than a decade of violence that some insist on calling the Taiping War in recognition of the awful damage it did to China, and that led to more deaths than the First World War. Promulgating a bizarre mixture of revolutionary fervour and Christian dogma, the Taiping rebels' leader was precisely the sort of enemy that China's indignity had created. Having failed the civil service entrance exams on several occasions, he woke up one morning and proclaimed that he was the son of God, waving pamphlets that he had picked up from a Christian missionary. His revolutionary movement, attracting the poor and dispossessed to his banner, would later be regarded as a forerunner of Communism, although none of its supposed higher aims were achieved before the Taiping rebels were wiped out with cataclysmic loss of life.

Much to the embarrassment of the Chinese, the British took over parts of local government during the crisis. Even though Shanghai was in the grip of the Taipings, British customs officials continued to run trade in the area, collecting taxes on behalf of the impotent Chinese government. Incidents such as this would later be used to twist the arm of the government in Beijing, stripping it day by day of its powers and responsibilities, until the maritime customs authority of China was entirely ceded to foreigners.

With the Russians pushing from the North, the Taipings uncontrollable in the South and other foreign powers boasting that they could bring China to heel when the imperial household could not, violence came to Beijing itself. When it arrived, it did so in the form of European aggression, as the demand for more trade and diplomacy was delivered out of the barrel of a gun. In August 1860, a force of some two hundred ships and seventeen thousand Europeans landed at Tianjin. They sent a delegation ahead to Beijing in the hope of negotiating a truce, but the Manchu general Sengge Rinchen ordered the emissaries to be tortured to death.

In October 1860, the combined French and British forces marched on the Summer Palace, expecting that the Xianfeng Emperor would be there. He and his entourage had already fled north to Jehol, leaving the new arrivals to wander, quite stunned, through the priceless artefacts of the gardens and palaces. Determined to punish the Chinese ruling class, rather than their people, for Sengge's atrocities, the British leader Lord Elgin ordered for the destruction of the Summer Palace. The Europeans took everything they could carry, smashing and burning whatever was left behind. Captain Charles Gordon, a young engineer with the British forces, reported that 'after pillaging it, [we] burned the whole place, destroying in a Vandal-like manner most valuable property ... It was wretchedly demoralising work for an army. Everybody was wild for plunder.' Two days later, Elgin ordered for the gutted buildings to be burned. A witness, Reverend R. J. L. McGhee, wrote:

> Out burst a hundred flames, the smoke obscures the
> sun, and temples, palaces, buildings and all, hallowed
> by age, if age can be hallow, and by beauty, if it can
> make sacred, are swept to destruction. A pang of
> sorrow seizes upon you ... No eye will ever gaze on
> those buildings ... records of by-gone skill and taste, of

which the world contains not the like. You have seen
them once and for ever ... man cannot reproduce them.

Antiques and plunder from the Summer Palace flowed
onto the European market, with bargain-hunters snatching
up little bits of chinoiserie, even as they tutted at the behaviour of the French and English. The event remains a cause
célèbre in Chinese history, recurring in documentaries
and fiction as an example of the terrible damage wrought
upon sovereign China by colonialists. Its most impressive
manifestation is Liu Yang's book *Who Collects the Yuan
Ming Yuan?*, a slab-like coffee-table tome that attempts to
reassemble the lost palace tile by tile, by tracking down its
pilfered remnants in museums, hotel lobbies and private
collections all around the world. When the bronze heads
of several zodiacal sculptures came on the global antique
market in the twenty-first century, wealthy Chinese businessmen bought them back for the nation.

What is often not mentioned is how much the ruinous
state of the Summer Palace owes to the Chinese themselves.
The great dissenter here is Hope Danby, whose *The Garden
of Perfect Brightness: The History of the Yuan Ming Yuan
and the Emperors Who Lived There* is full of correctives,
including the claim that the fabled zodiac animals were
actually removed twenty years before the attack, at the
order of an empress who hated them. This, however, still
does not explain how some of them turned up in a Beverly
Hills swimming pool a century later – at the time Danby
was writing, she assumed they had been melted down.

It was the Manchu imperial family who decided to leave

the Old Summer Palace derelict, and the Chinese common people who spent the next century sneaking over the walls to plunder it for any remaining statues, tiles and even bricks that they could find to re-use in housebuilding. According to Jasper Becker in *City of Heavenly Tranquillity*, this continued assault on the gardens went on as late as 1969, when citizens were raiding the Summer Palace for bricks to use in bomb shelters. The Summer Palace remained a location for squatters' housing and fly-tipping for the rest of the twentieth century – its modern role as an icon of wronged China is very recent indeed.

The burning of the Summer Palace was yet one more sign of the end of the empire. The Xianfeng Emperor, nominal ruler of China, died aged just thirty, leaving a child as his successor. Meanwhile, the new emperor's regents reluctantly agreed to the ultimate insult – the presence of foreign legation buildings in Beijing itself, in a Legation Quarter just to the south of the Forbidden City. Beijing, and China itself, came to be regarded by the foreign powers in much the way that they regarded its six-year-old Tongzhi Emperor: as an ineffectual child that needed to have its responsibilities shouldered by others until it was able to fend for itself.

The Origin of 'Peking'
The word 'Peking', which means nothing to the Chinese, carries within it at least part of the story of the foreign guests. When Lord Macartney came to China in 1793, he recorded the name of China's capital in his journal as 'Pekin'. Thomas Wade, a former ambassador who ended his days as Cambridge's first professor of Chinese, published

the first English-language textbook of Chinese in 1867. Wade developed a system for Romanising Chinese sounds during his long career in the diplomatic service, encompassing large amounts of time far to the south in Hong Kong, where the local dialect was much harsher and more guttural. The word 'Beijing' was hence written in Wade's syllabary as 'Peking'. He expected the P to be pronounced as a B, and the K to be pronounced as J. To actually make the sound 'Peking' with Wade's syllabary, a linguist would need to add apostrophe-like voice markers and write it 'P'e k'ing'.

Needless to say, this spelling, particularly as codified later on by Herbert Giles to form the Wade-Giles orthography, has eternally confused the non-specialist as to Chinese pronunciations. Matters were not helped by variation in pronunciation within China itself. Down in the South, where so many British visitors were concentrated in Hong Kong, the local language pronounced Beijing as something more like 'Bakging', which actually made the Wade-Giles rendering make more sense than it ought to. The confusion would continue for half of the twentieth century, until Communist China, determined to free itself from the shackles of imperialist influences – even in the writing of its own language – approved the creation of its own Romanisation system in 1958. The new system, which writes Beijing as 'Beijing', was not officially introduced until 1979, hence explaining the common discrepancy between generations. I grew up hearing the word 'Beijing', reinforced when I began studying Chinese under teachers from Mainland China. My parents' generation grew up hearing 'Peking', and many of them have yet to shake it off.

The Empress Dowager

Regardless of the activities of the foreigners, it is often said that China's worst enemy in the latter half of the nineteenth century was a young widow of the Xianfeng Emperor, who would serve in various capacities as a regent for her son and then her nephew. Her most common name today is Cixi (1835–1908), but she is often known by the title that she initially received as the mother of Xianfeng's successor: the Empress Dowager. There is no statue of her; despite her immense celebrity and world fame in her lifetime, the Chinese are understandably reluctant to commemorate her.

Only twenty-six years old at the time of her husband's death, the Empress Dowager would dominate Chinese politics for the next forty years. Then as now, it is the Empress Dowager, a cosseted concubine turned grande dame, who is most often held responsible for the spectacular demise of imperial China. This is, perhaps, unfair. Chinese folklore speaks of an ancient curse predicting that a woman of Cixi's clan would destroy the empire, but it seems overly simplistic to blame a twenty-six-year-old woman for China's failure to hold off foreign predators and domestic revolution. In the early years of her reign, the Empress Dowager had more pressing matters at hand – being forced to share the power of the regency with noblemen administrators and the late emperor's chief wife. Cixi was only a concubine and received a position in the hierarchy solely for being the birth mother of the new emperor. Cixi may have been pigheaded, but she was a creation of centuries of stultifying tradition. She was barely literate – an extant edict in her own handwriting botches many characters – and wholly ignorant of the challenges that China would face if it were to square up to foreign pressure.

In 1872, her son came of age, supposedly bringing an end to the regency. But the reign of this Tongzhi Emperor lasted a mere three years, as he embarked on a series of ill-advised schemes, including an expensive attempt to repair the Summer Palace, and the demotion of many administrators who had annoyed him during the regency. Dead by 1875, allegedly of syphilis picked up in the brothels of Dazhalan, the Tongzhi Emperor left no heir of his own, prompting Cixi to adopt her three-year-old nephew, proclaim a new regency and thereby buy herself another generation in power.

Cixi infamously used money earmarked for the modernisation of the Imperial Navy to renovate her holiday homes at the Summer Palace – hence the distinction in modern maps between the 'Old' palace, which is still in ruins, and the 'New'.

The shoreline of Kunming Lake still features the most notorious of the results – a marble terrace in the shape of a stylised paddle steamer, constructed at the Empress Dowager's order to give her another idyllic spot for moonlit banquets. It is an intricate, beautiful folly – in every sense of the word – and an enduring monument to Cixi's blinkered grasp on reality, embodying a fortune squandered on a playful garden ornament at a time when China's military struggled to hold off ironclad foreign warships with antique wooden galleons.

It is easy to laugh at Cixi's frivolity, but some might argue that the renovation of the Summer Palace was not a bitch-queen's bid for luxury at all, but a desperate attempt by some of her officials to get her out of the way. For decades, factions in the Forbidden City sought to lure Cixi out of power with the one tool available to them: the good life. In one famous incident, palace officials waited until Cixi had expressly ordered that she not be disturbed during an opera performance, before taking advantage of the strict prohibition to pass and carry out an order of execution against one of her cronies. Similarly, we might suppose that administrators hoped to lure her out of Beijing so that others might be able to get on with the business of running the country – the Summer Palace is now a mere subway stop on Line 4, but a hundred years ago was half a day's ride outside the city. Whether these men would have done a better job of holding off disaster, we will never know; their ruses never quite worked, and Cixi remained in charge.

No new ships were bought for the Chinese navy after 1888, leading to a humiliating defeat in the First Sino–Japanese War, of 1894–5, when Japanese incursion into Korea was met with brave-but-futile Chinese military intervention. As the Manchus clung to past glories, hiring officials on the basis of their family connections or mastery of classical texts, modern achievements in engineering and technology were changing the world. Beneath the notice of the Manchus, the history of North China was fast becoming tied to the fortunes of the railway that the Russians had built across Eurasia. With the establishment on the Pacific of Vladivostok – a port whose name ominously translates as 'domination of the East' – the Russian Empire could now move men and materiel swiftly to and from the Pacific. The

Chinese had little say in the movement of Russian trains both around and through the Manchurian homeland of the imperial family; instead, the nearby island of Japan offered the strongest resistance. Seeing themselves as the 'British of Asia', the Japanese desired to be regarded as equals of the Western imperialists – which, for them, meant swiftly modernising and then demanding similar concessions in China to those received by the Europeans.

Meanwhile, the foreign legations took over an entire city sector, perilously close to the Forbidden City. Today, the city blocks behind and to the east of the National Museum, stretching all the way from Tiananmen to Wangfujing, often reward the wanderer with sights of forgotten consulate gates and foreigner-built banks, long since repurposed as Chinese Communist Party branches and offices.

The invaders brought foreign ideas – a railway from Tianjin edged into the city by 1896, scandalously requiring the knocking down of a patch of wall, and a pitiful few Chinese and Manchu court officials attempted some reforms to strengthen China. They did so in the name of her charge, the Guangxu Emperor, leading the Empress Dowager to effectively dismiss him – although still nominally the Son of Heaven, he was kept sequestered in a palace while his supporters were rounded up and executed.

Beyond the walls of the Forbidden City, there was a rift across China between the small ruling class of Manchus, and the great masses of ethnic Chinese. Running low on friends, some among the Manchus fatally offered tacit support to one of the few uprisings that aimed to oust 'foreigners' without including the Manchus in their number.

After further signs of Heaven's displeasure – flooding in 1898, then droughts in 1899 and 1900 – a society calling itself Yihe Quan ('the righteous and harmonious fist') rose up, supposedly to defend Chinese tradition from unwelcome foreign influences. Made famous by innumerable movies in the ensuing century, these 'Boxers' preached a form of martial art that purported to make its adherents invulnerable to bullets. Although this was soon proved to be untrue, the Boxer movement grew in stature, until armies of anti-foreign militia roamed China in search of missionaries and merchants to murder.

They reached Beijing in June 1900, at first in small groups, easily marked out by their red headbands and belts. What with the dust and the heat, observed the British journalist Putnam Weale, June was 'the historic month which has seen more crises than any other'. By 8 June, the embassy district was worried enough at reports of attacks on foreigners in Beijing to request permission for more soldiers to be brought up from Tianjin for their own protection. On 11 June, the Boxers struck close to home, murdering a Japanese diplomat ahead of a mass Boxer invasion two days later.

The first Boxer assault on the legations was repelled with a few gunshots. The following week, one of the Empress Dowager's wilier officials leaked a forged document that claimed that the foreigners had demanded the right to take over all administration in China. The angry Boxers struck back in their thousands, trapping the foreigners and their families in the Legation Quarter in an armed siege that lasted for several weeks.

The siege of the foreign legations achieved worldwide

infamy, uniting newspapers in Europe, America and Japan in their horror of the way foreigners were treated in China. It was an offence to the tender sensibilities of the Christian world, which regarded the activities of missionaries in China as sacrosanct, and the foreign media was soon rife with stories of brave soldiers fighting off sword-waving Boxer rebels and devout missionary matrons cowering before rapacious rebels.

In a footnote to the violence, Weale recorded an attempt by the besieged legations to dig under their own buildings to fight off Chinese sappers. Ten feet below the surface, the European diggers found scores of cannonballs, which they presumed to have fallen upon what was once open fields in the days of the Mongol invasion.

> In other places, splendid drains have been bared –
> drains four feet high and three broad, which run
> everywhere. Once, when Marco Polo was young,
> Peking must have been a fit and proper place, and the
> magnificent streets magnificently clean. Now...!

It was not until 14 August that a relief force arrived in the city, with Russians, British and Japanese racing for the chance to be the first on the scene. In fact, it was a Sikh soldier with the British army who was the first into the besieged area, crawling through a filthy sewer gate and along a ditch to announce the arrival of rescuers to the surviving residents. Chinese residents of Beijing had fled in their thousands, fearing the foreigners even more than the marauding Boxers. Cixi herself, disguised in peasant clothes, had been one of the anonymous figures in the retreating throng, abandoning the city from which her clan supposedly ruled the world.

While the relief of the legations was a feel-good story all over the Western world, the incident spelled disaster for Beijing and its surroundings. The city was partitioned between the rescuing forces, which imposed harsh military order on any Chinese who had not already fled the city. Beijing was divided under stern American-British-Japanese martial law for the following year, while the occupiers refused to negotiate with the Manchus until the Empress Dowager herself returned from hiding. The concept of Most Favoured Nation status even extended to plunder – German troops arrived late for the fighting, but still received a sector of the city.

The ensuing weeks saw Beijing torn apart by its new owners. Boxers broke into the Summer Palace, under renovation after the Europeans' earlier looting, and raided the new buildings for timber. Back in town, entrepreneurs wrenched the famous astronomical instruments from the roof of the Old Observatory and sent them to Germany, where they stayed for more than a decade, until the Germans were obliged to give them back in the aftermath of the First World War.

The Empress Dowager did not return with her court until January 1902, when she arrived by train in what could have been a symbolic gesture of defeat. Instead, her arrival seems to have been regarded with elation by many of the Europeans present. When she offered them a little bow as she passed, they burst into applause. A similar selective amnesia about her involvement in anti-foreigner movements seemed to extend to the settlement over the incident, which left the Empress Dowager herself largely unaffected, although several of her officials were forced to take responsibility for the sequence of events, and they paid with their lives.

But it was too late. The Manchus would never recover from the Boxer Rebellion. Russian incursions into the north-west, originally undertaken in the name of restoring order, were slow to retreat, leading eventually to the Russo–Japanese War of 1904–5 that saw Japan victorious and the czar's authority fatally undermined. Reluctantly, the Manchus began preparations to modernise, sending a delegation to the West to learn its ways, although conservative opposition was still so strong that a suicide bomber attacked the delegates as they prepared to leave Beijing.

The Guangxu Emperor, still in seclusion, and the Empress Dowager both died in 1908, so close to each other that foul play was long suspected. The ailing Cixi ordered her eunuchs to carry her in a litter to Guangxu's chambers, where the two fading adversaries stared wordlessly at each other in a final seething farewell. It was not until 2008, on the centenary of the emperor's death, that *China Daily* reported high concentrations of arsenic being found in Guangxu's corpse.

Guangxu was succeeded by his nephew, another powerless infant, who screamed and wailed at his coronation until his father tried to soothe him with the fateful words, 'Don't worry, this will soon be over.' The toddler's reign title was announced as Xuantong ('proclamation'), perhaps implying a hope that China would soon be reformed by a series of imperial fiats. But he is better known today as 'Henry' Puyi, the Last Emperor.

6

Northern Peace: 1912–1949

His picture is everywhere. His face stares thoughtfully on every banknote, from one yuan up. His statues and silhouettes clog every bric-a-brac shop and market stall. His giant portrait graces the front of the Tiananmen gate itself, gazing across the square like a serene Buddha in a featureless grey jacket. Every October, it is replaced with a fresh portrait that looks exactly the same.

The man himself, or what's left of him, is on the south side of the square, deep within the building that unkind critics have described as resembling an unimaginative gymnasium. Although Mao Zedong (1893–1976) had tried to get all Party grandees to agree to cremation, he was overruled after his death, and laid to rest in this mausoleum. His body, carefully embalmed and pickled, spends each night in a downstairs freezer, before being hydraulically raised back to its position in front of the troops of pious mourners.

There is no need to be daunted by the queue. Nobody can pause, so the long line shuffles through with relative speed. Visitors to China may even feel a sense of elation upon realising this is the only place in the entire nation where one's passage will not be impeded by some buffoon with a selfie stick. After you have swiftly been ushered through to pay your respects, you enter another chamber, decorated with the massive characters of a famous poem written by Mao in 1961, the 'Reply to Comrade Guo Moruo'.

Mired in a complex discussion of whether or not a play about one of the mythical Monkey King's battles contained allusions to China's relationship with Soviet Russia, the poem appears to have been reproduced here for Mao's apparent identification of himself with the bold, impetuous Monkey King, cutting through the illusions that arise in a terrible storm, seeing the terrible white-boned demon that bears down upon him and sweeping enemies from the sky like dust.

It is this version of Mao that is commemorated in his mausoleum – the great helmsman who worked miracles, leading a revolution from a desert cave and sweeping to power as the People's champion. Little is said about the Mao of the last twenty years of his life – the bitter, petulant mastermind of putsches and purges, the deluded visionary who led his people into cataclysmic experiments in social engineering that cost millions of lives.

The 100-Day Empire
'Here we are in Peking at last,' wrote Ellen LaMotte, 'the beautiful, barbaric capital of China, the great, gorgeous capital of Asia. For Peking is the capital of Asia, or the whole Orient, the centre of the stormy politics of the Far East.'

Revolution had been brewing for decades, nurtured by overseas communities of Chinese, by secret societies that claimed to have been lying in wait since the fall of the Ming dynasty, and encouraged by democratic movements abroad.

When revolution came to China, it came to the fractious south. Beijing, power centre for the old order, was slow to fall into step with the times.

Although the Last Emperor was still supposedly the ruler of All Under Heaven, by 1912 he ruled only within his palace. Beijing itself was under the control of Yuan Shikai, an aging military man who had been called out of retirement in an attempt to keep order in the city. Yuan still had an army, and he offered such an implacable resistance to the revolutionaries in the South that they were often obliged to play along with him. Although Sun Yatsen is remembered as the first president of Republican China, he was in power only for a matter of days before he grudgingly resigned his post in favour of Yuan.

China hovered on the brink of fragmentation as several provinces toyed with the possibility of proclaiming their own independence. But while the notions of democracy and Republicanism were strong in some places, in Beijing it seemed possible that the fall of the Manchus would merely lead to a new imperial dynasty. Yuan was declared president for a five-year term, soon extended to ten, and by 1915 he began preparations to become even more powerful.

It had been more than a decade since the last sacrificial rites were performed at the Altar of Heaven. Yuan eventually agreed to perform the rites himself, in a failed bid to establish himself as the new emperor. He proclaimed himself as Hongxian ('overwhelming constitution'), but his shambolic reign lasted for a mere 100 days.

Many histories paint Yuan Shikai as a corrupt official, but his defenders insist that he was a loyal statesman frantically attempting to drag China into the twentieth century by the most efficient constitutional means – if he demanded coronation, they say, then it was merely because the Chinese people did not understand the concept of political power that did not derive from a mandate of Heaven. China had seen many dynasties come and go, and it would not have been the first time that a warlord had marched into Beijing, toppled the incumbent dynasty and then proclaimed his own. Republican and Nationalist rhetoric, with all its talk of democracy, may not have trickled down to the man in the street, particularly when the concept appeared so foreign.

It is only now, a century after the event, that we know the Qing dynasty to have truly fallen. In 1912, many would have still expected, or hoped, or dreaded that some form of restoration might occur, either in full or in some sort of compromise that offered the Last Emperor a form of constitutional monarchy.

Yuan Shikai's government ordered that the Great Qing Gate, opposite Tiananmen, the Gate of Heavenly Peace, should be renamed the Great China Gate, removing the tablet on its eaves that associated the name of the edifice with that of the departed dynasty. But workmen were scrupulously careful as they removed its sign, deciding that it would be unwise to destroy the Great Qing sign, since there was no way of telling at that moment whether the dynasty was truly over. Hedging their bets, they decided to wrap it carefully against knocks and scrapes and to stow it out of harm's way in the gate's attic, ready for a swift Orwellian reversal of nomenclature in the event of a sudden restoration. As they moved the sign to a suitably undisturbed corner, they found another tablet of similar size and shape, obscured beneath centuries of dust and grime. The writing on it read 'Great Ming' – it had been stashed in a similar fashion in the seventeenth century by their predecessors.

The 4 May Movement

Impoverished China stood little chance of making a meaningful military contribution to the Allied Powers fighting in the First World War. Japanese diplomats attempted to impose a series of invasive deals that would turn parts of China into a Japanese colony, leading China's own statesmen to fight back with a cunning ruse. China offered the Allied Powers 'labourers in place of soldiers', sending some 140,000 workers to Europe to dig trenches, clear battlefields and work in factories, freeing up able-bodied European men to fight against Germany. This ensured China a place at the negotiating table at the end of the war and, it was hoped, would prevent its Japanese 'ally' taking advantage of the fall of Germany's colonies in China by occupying them itself.

The end of the First World War saw jubilant celebrations in Beijing. It was widely believed that the defeat of Germany would see the restoration of Shandong province to China and with it, one might presume, the removal of any need for other foreign powers to keep up their bases on other parts of Chinese soil. The mood of the times, at least, suggested that the foreigners would now begin their retreat from China. However, many of the partygoers in the Beijing streets were unaware that Shandong had already been sold out, offered as security on a 20-million-yen loan from Japan. When the subject of Shandong came up at the Paris Peace Conference, the Chinese were scandalised to hear that the German territory would be 'restored' not to China, but to the Japanese who had occupied it.

Protests broke out over both the loan itself and the perceived betrayal of Chinese interests; celebrants in front of the Tiananmen gate were replaced with student demonstrators. Whipped into a frenzy, they turned east towards the old Legation Quarter, where they planned on attacking the Japanese embassy. Armed guards presented too imposing a threat to the crowds, so they turned towards a new target. Instead of lynching the Japanese ambassador, they attacked the house of the Chinese minister of communications, whom they rightly suspected had been a prime broker in the Shandong scandal.

The fact that a paltry number of guards was able to frighten them away from the Japanese embassy speaks volumes. Although there were thousands of demonstrators, the number of active militants was considerably fewer – at first, only thirty-two arrests were made. Regardless, news of the incident spread throughout China and found support in many other cities. In Beijing itself, it was followed by strikes and a boycott of Japanese goods. Although the initial troublemakers had already been released, further demonstrations seemed much more wide-ranging – there were three thousand arrests, until the prisons of Beijing were overflowing. In June, Chinese diplomats refused to sign the Treaty of Versailles.

This protest, on 4 May 1919, became enshrined in later annals as a crucial moment in the history of Chinese

Communism. It was, the Party historians later claimed, a moment when the Chinese people had had enough and turned on the government toadies who had betrayed their trust. The fact that the protest happened in front of the Gate of Heavenly Peace, in the area we know better today as Tiananmen Square, was to make later Chinese governments incredibly jumpy at the sight of student protesters in the same place. The 4 May incident was a landmark in the history of Beijing and the history of China, but for some it also set a dangerous precedent. The uprising established student radicals as prime influences on decision-making and brought the authority of the Republican government into disrepute. It is no coincidence that a Communist youth group was founded in Beijing by 1920.

Meanwhile, Beijing lost its status as capital once more. The shaky Republican state in the south proclaimed that Nanjing, the 'south capital', was the new centre of the Chinese government. Beijing, perilously close to Russian and Japanese interests and the Manchurian heartland, had fallen out of fashion and was renamed yet again. With a degree of blind faith, it was called Beiping, or Northern Peace.

The years that followed saw the city buffeted by the interests of local warlords, resurgent Republicans and Japanese intrigues. 'War and rumours arrived like clockwork,' wrote the novelist Lao She in *Rickshaw Boy*, 'every year during planting season.' Manchuria itself, homeland of the Qing dynasty, fell under Japanese control and became a puppet regime ruled by the Last Emperor – he might have lost China, but he clung to Manchuria for a while longer.

In 1926, demonstrators gathered in front of the Tiananmen gate to protest about the warlord Zhang Zuolin, who had caved to Japanese demands over Manchuria. Armed police shot and killed forty-seven of them, wounding hundreds more. The writer Lu Xun saw it as a sign of things to come. 'This is not the conclusion of an incident,' he wrote, 'but a new beginning. Lies written in ink can never disguise facts written in blood. All blood debts must be repaid in kind.' Sure enough, it was not the last time that Tiananmen would be witness to a standoff between governors and governed.

Paul French, in his evocative *Midnight in Peking*, notes that 'between 1916 and 1928 alone, no fewer than seven warlord rulers came and went ... They and their ilk terrorised the city as they bled it dry.' The city was awash with soldiers and refugees, bandits-turned-militia and victims of the distant Russian Revolution. Such straitened, lawless times brought dangers of their own to the city's heritage, offering irresistible temptations to the burglar and the pilferer and threatening many heritage items and locales. As Arlington and Lewisohn noted in their book *In Search of Old Peking*:

> One might, perhaps, pass over minor acts of vandalism, such as converting historic palaces into modern restaurants and tea-houses; famous temples into barracks and police stations; cutting down ancient cypresses to sell for firewood; defacing age-old walls and tablets with political slogans, and so forth. But in many instances, historical buildings and monuments have actually been destroyed by official orders.

Up near today's Lama Temple is one of Beijing's few surviving pailou – commemorative archways, familiar to foreigner visitors from their duplicates in many a Chinatown. Once, such memorial arches were everywhere, 'emblazoned all over with gilded characters and sprawling dragons [to] honour some great Chinese – erected to his memory instead of a library or a hospital or something like that', wrote Ellen La Motte in 1916. Almost all of them were pulled down in the next thirty years.

In 1937, trouble broke out over a seemingly minor incident at the Marco Polo Bridge, when Japanese officers demanded to be let into a fortified town nearby to search for a missing member of their company. Chinese soldiers refused, and the Japanese advanced across the bridge with tanks on 8 July. Chinese forces retook the bridge the day after and later agreed tentative terms with the Japanese, in which the soldiers agreed not to advance further. Despite this, Japanese tanks were in Beijing by 29 July – supposedly to defend the interests of the city's Japanese businessmen and residents.

North-east China had become a Japanese vassal, and the Second Sino–Japanese War had begun. Although it started as a conflict between Japanese occupiers and Nationalist Chinese defenders in Beijing and other occupied zones, mainly along the coast, the war would escalate until 1941, when the Japanese attack on Pearl Harbor brought the Allied forces into the conflict on the side of the Chinese.

Beijing's antiquities suffered a predictable degree of neglect during the period. With no imperial family left to even consider maintaining the Summer Palace, its ruins fell even further into disrepair, raided for building materials by desperate locals and even gaining a small cluster of shanty towns. The end of the war would not lead to reconstruction. The Japanese might have left, but the city was still in a dilapidated state and suffered all the more when a new conflict broke out. The Chinese Communists and Chinese Nationalists, who had worked under a fragile treaty during the Japanese occupation, now turned on each other.

The Communists enjoyed strong support in the countryside, where local peasants often remembered comparatively few sightings of Nationalists during the campaigns against the Japanese. Before long, the civil war saw the Nationalists chased out of China, retreating to the offshore island of Taiwan, which retains a Nationalist (i.e. non-Communist) Chinese government to this day.

The People's Republic of China
In October 1949, Chairman Mao stood at the balcony of the Tiananmen gate and proclaimed, 'The Chinese people, comprising one quarter of humanity, have now stood up.' He spoke to a crowd who had seen the worst of China's civil war. Tellingly, their various hurrahs still bore the taint of the imperial age, wishing Mao 'ten thousand years' as if he were a new emperor. Modern propaganda carefully rewrites the sense of it – the huge words on the gate today co-opt the idea for all, and not a single person. 'Ten thousand years to the great unity of the world's peoples,' they read, before the line is broken by a massive portrait of Mao. The line continues on the other side, 'Ten thousand years to the People's Republic of China.'

Never quite self-sufficient, Beijing had been cruelly tortured by the disruption of its food supply from the Nationalist South. Shortages had taken their toll in the closing days of the war, while money had been rendered meaningless by inflation at 8,000 per cent. The nominal restoration of the city's status as a capital had meant nothing under Japanese occupation. It did not become fashionable to call it Beijing again until 1949, and the city had been marginalised during a crucial two decades of technological development. A handful of main thoroughfares had been paved and smeared with rudimentary tarmac, but they had long since crumbled beneath years of neglect, the heavy rumble of military vehicles and the inevitable consequences of Beijing's icy winters. The rest of the town was little changed from the days of the Boxers – more than two-thirds of the residents still drew their water from wells, and few homes had electricity. The previous winter, people had been dying in the Beijing streets, with sweepers reporting 200 individuals fatally frozen or starved in a single district. Those who made it to January 1949 were forced to endure a series of purges, as the victorious Communists hunted down thousands of Nationalist sympathisers and deserters in the city.

With old money only available in ludicrously high denominations, or bearing the unwelcome faces of pre-Revolution rulers, traders were forbidden to use anything but the new Communist notes. More pragmatic residents turned to barter or the black market, and money itself fell out of fashion. Some form of rationing, of either certain basic foodstuffs or certain textiles, remained in force for another thirty years.

The surviving palaces of the Manchu era were transformed into homes and offices for the Party faithful. Mao himself took up residence in the luxurious Zhongnanhai pleasure park to the west of the Forbidden City. But Mao and his associates had arrived in Beijing after years of deprivation as guerrillas in the wilderness. They had lived lives of relative austerity – even when able to put down roots in their Yan'an headquarters, they were essentially living in caves. Since many, including Mao himself, came from peasant backgrounds to begin with, they brought a new and radically uncomplicated attitude towards the city. Beijing in the early days of the Communist era still retained vestiges of its imperial grandeur, enough for Soviet advisers in the 1950s to develop a reputation as shopaholics and bargain hunters. But Mao would soon put a stop to that.

Much of China's imperial treasure had already been spirited away to safety by the fleeing Nationalists, at first stored in vaults by the government-in-exile at Chongqing. After the war, the treasures were relocated to Taiwan, where they remain today in one of the most richly appointed museums in the world. Their continued presence there remains a matter of Chinese diplomatic embarrassment, comparable to a similar argument of preservation and ownership to be heard between Britain and Greece over the Elgin Marbles. The chief difference is in the rhetoric – the governments in Taipei and Beijing both claim to be the rulers of China and hence the most appropriate guardians of the antiquities. To this day, many priceless relics of Beijing's history are in the National Palace Museum in Taipei, the subjects of recurring quarrels between the rival governments.

7

Empty Spaces: 1949–1989

You won't find her in Beijing. She was torn down and pulverised in swift order on a June day in 1989. But her sisters have sprung up in many places outside China. One of the most solid and enduring examples appeared at the heart of San Francisco's Chinatown in 1994. There, in Portsmouth Square, a bronze statue still holds a flaming torch aloft. Any resemblance the Goddess of Democracy bears to the Statue of Liberty is purely coincidental; according to participants in the original construction, the students who created her based their work more on Soviet models than anything so provocatively pro-American.

The Beijing original was 33 feet tall, fabricated in a hurry from papier-mâché pieces over a metal armature. She had angular, almost Manchu features, and hair that seemed to be blowing in an imaginary storm. She was originally erected in an act and a place of defiance, raising her torch and scowling right across the road at the portrait of Mao on the front of the Tiananmen bastion. Today, there is very little evidence in Tiananmen Square that she was ever there. You can only sense her by her absence, by the large numbers of soldiers, police and conspicuous plain-clothes security details on permanent vigil, and by the restrictions that turn simply crossing the road into an elaborate exercise in kettling and queuing. This, in a very post-modern sense, is a place where a statue once was, and it is only one of the most recent of Beijing's many, many monumental absences.

Permanent Revolution

Mao's grand scheme for Beijing was like his plan for China itself: a state of permanent revolution, deliberately defying tradition. The most noticeable casualty was the city wall. At first, the damage was minor. Taking a leaf from the foreign railway builders of the nineteenth century, the town planners of Beijing smashed broad gaps in the old wall to allow better transport access. In the age of intercontinental ballistic missiles, there seemed little point in having such a small barrier to the outside world. 'Tradition' itself was a dirty word – 'tradition' meant centuries of imperial despotism, the suppression of the workers, the enslavement of women. Particularly strong in the early 1950s, when things were still friendly with Soviet Russia, was the desire to emulate Soviet modernism. This was most obvious of all in what had come to be called Tiananmen Square, created by clearing a space around the approach road to the Forbidden City, deliberately designed as a rival to Red Square in Moscow, and dominated by the giant column of the Monument to the People's Heroes.

Following Soviet Russia's example, China under Mao threw itself into vast, strenuous national initiatives, beginning with the first Five-Year Plan. Beijing, with its unreliable water and distant fuel supply, was unsuitable for large-scale industrialisation, but Mao was determined to turn it into a factory-workers' city like Moscow. Many Beijing buildings were pulled down and replaced with brutalist state architecture, but nothing quite so brutal as the troubles that would follow among the Chinese themselves.

Fortunately, Beijing had a saviour of sorts in the form of Liang Sicheng (1901–72), an architectural historian who championed much of what passed for preservation of its pre-Communist heritage. Realising that the rest of China would take its cue from whatever was implemented in the capital, he regarded Beijing as the crucial model for architectural and town-planning policy. As vice-director for the Beijing City Planning Commission, he argued that the very centre of town, the old Manchu city, should be devoid of all industry, in order to spare it congestion and pollution. In a prophetic gesture that showed him to be years ahead of his time, he argued for the long-term heritage value of the Forbidden City and demanded that it should be preserved in its imperial-era form. Moreover, to maintain the majesty of traditional Beijing, he ordered that no buildings within the compass of the old city walls should be more than three storeys high.

Liang visualised Beijing as a monument to itself, a living museum that included a grand central axis of contemporary government buildings as well as lovingly preserved commemorations of the imperial past. 'We have inherited this priceless and unique historical property,' he wrote. 'How can we now destroy it?' It is Liang we have to thank for the 'Chinesey' quality of many of Beijing's streets; insisting that buildings in China should have a sense of national character, he encouraged even skyscrapers to have traditional up-curved roof structures to evoke the ancient past.

He did not win all of his battles. Despite his passionate defence of the last of the pailou commemorative gates and the historical significance of the old city walls and gates, he was forced to watch as Party cadres authorised their demolition. In one case, that of the picturesque gate Xizhimen, officials sped up the process by first arranging for it to catch fire, so it could then be condemned as a hazardous ruin. Liang likened his experience of the destruction of the city's heritage as feeling that he personally was being flayed alive.

Although the Nationalist Chinese were gone, it did not follow that all was well. The Korean War plunged China back into a conflict on its own doorstep, while the Nationalist regime in Taiwan continued to boast that it would soon return to take back China from the Communists.

There was argument within the ranks of the Communists themselves – some supported the Soviet Russian model; others argued that there were unique conditions in China that required a uniquely Chinese solution. Further confusion broke out when it was revealed that the Russians themselves were in disagreement. In 1956, Nikita Khrushchev scandalised the Communist world by denouncing the late Joseph Stalin, on whose personality cult Mao had modelled his own. It led Mao to invite denunciations of his own, via his Hundred Flowers Campaign – which encouraged criticism of Communist progress – only to turn on his critics with the purges that followed.

The tenth anniversary of the People's Republic saw ten great architectural projects put in place, including the Great Hall of the People that dominates the western side of Tiananmen Square. Liang Sicheng had hoped that much of the country's administrative hub would be built further outside the city, but he had already fallen out of favour and had little say in the new super-projects. But despite being the capital again and serving as a home to the Party leadership, Beijing lagged far behind many other towns in terms of its industrial production.

In an attempt to stave off the droughts and water shortages that had been a perennial feature of Beijing life from the time of the legendary dragons, the Communist leadership decided to build a new dam up near the tombs of the Ming emperors. Massive 'voluntary' public labour ensured that the dam was completed within six months, although it would appear that Communist engineers relied more on blind faith than they may have been prepared to admit. Once complete, the dam created a reservoir that is still rarely full – nobody had dared point out that many of the rivers flowing into it were dry for much of the year. Such gigantic but fruitless projects became a feature of the early Communist era, with much wasted effort, wasted time and wasted lives.

Another project, the Miyun Reservoir, had greater success, taming two rivers that were often prone to flooding, and creating a new water supply for Beijing. But even Miyun was not trouble-free – much of the early work was almost washed away during rainstorms in 1959, and early plans to use excess water to create a navigable canal were abandoned in time.

At the Summer Palace, there began a slow process of restoration – Kunming Lake was returned to its former function as a staging post for aqueducts into Beijing proper, while the surrounding area was reinvented as a public park. The ruins of the European assaults were left as they were, allowing the Party faithful to reflect upon the implications of a weak China and foreign aggression.

The worst damage would come in the 1960s, when a China drunk on modernism decided to do away entirely with the walls of the Manchu city. They were pulled down to make space for a combined ring road and subway. Those pre-Communist buildings that survive in Beijing are lucky to have done so after years of warfare and a Soviet-inspired remodelling.

And then... a generation of children raised on the thoughts of Chairman Mao reached their rebellious teens and turned, in his name, on the Party itself. The Cultural Revolution, spearheaded by the fanatical Red Guards, sought to destroy much of what was left of old China. Many of those museums, temples and artefacts that had not been irreparably damaged in a century of unrest were destroyed in 1966. If it were not for the intercession of Premier Zhou Enlai, the Forbidden City and Beihai Park might also have been ruined.

This is why Dingling, the tomb of the Ming emperor Wanli, Emperor of 10,000 Experiences (1563–1620), is empty today. In the early days of Five-Year Plans, which were even applied to archaeological digs as if they were factories turning out artefacts, Dingling suffered at the hands of its excavators, who forged ahead without adequate measures in place to preserve the lavish silk garments and hangings to be found inside the tomb, many of which were left to rot in a damp shed. Matters were compounded by the outbreak of the Cultural Revolution, which not only suspended archaeological work but culminated in the invasion of the site by fanatic Red Guards, who dragged out the skeletons of Wanli and his concubines, denounced them – as if being dead were not punishment enough – and then set fire to them and their possessions.

Nobody would deny that putting hungry farmers and resentful teenagers in charge of national policy was bound to end in disaster, but there were other factors. Maoism's inventor was a man out of time – a peasant boy made good, undoubtedly bright, who studied hard to gain a Confucian education only to discover that he had been born in an era where his classical knowledge was next to useless in an age of railways and power stations. He spent the rest of his life making up for it, refusing to admit that newfangled knowledge required more than willpower to master. His country origins and his classical reading often gave his pronouncements a sort of homespun quality. To intellectuals, he could come across as pig-headed, ignorant or chillingly facetious. But to the masses he sounded like a plain-spoken man of the people, always ready with words of managerial encouragement, always on hand with a few blindly optimistic parables of the utopia to come. When running a guerrilla campaign in the wilderness, he found this was enough to inspire his troops on to victory. It was, however, no way to run a country. Blithe dismissal of scientific reality was less of an issue when there were no engines to start or combine harvesters to service. But similar denials of bad harvests and poor production were to plunge China into a secret famine that killed millions in the early days of Communism.

Mao himself falls in and out of fashion. The current Party line regards him as a necessary evil and an important icon of unity– a leader who dragged China up by its bootstraps, only to come unstuck when the war was done and the time for peaceful progress arrived. On his deathbed, he offered dire warnings about the future of Communism, reminding his successors that they would have to stick to their guns for the next generation, lest the achievements of Communism be undermined by the temptations of the Capitalist free market. When those temptations won over, they were forced through by a faction within the Party that clung to Mao's maxim that leaders should 'seek the truth from facts'. The facts, they argued, had changed. If Mao were alive now, he would be reacting differently.

Far from creating enduring edifices and artefacts to benefit the people, Mao's era often created little more than empty spaces – gaps where buildings should have been; the absence of joy and freedom; shortages of food and other necessities; a lost generation of doctors and engineers, exiled to the countryside to 'learn' from the peasants; and thousands upon thousands of people quietly made to disappear.

The Underground City
I thought it would be a journey like any other. I hailed a cab just outside the last remnant of the old city wall, by the newly restored watchtower. But when I asked the driver to take me to the Underground City, he suddenly lost the ability to understand me. I drew him the Chinese characters. He shook his head and all but kicked me out of his cab.

The next driver was a similar case. Initially, he was so

eager to snap up a rich foreign fare that he swerved across two lanes to get to me. But once I told him I wanted to go to the Underground City, he blinked blankly and said he had no idea what I was talking about. I pointed it out to him on the map, but he acted as if it weren't there. Eventually, we reached a compromise; I named the corner of a street that was *near* the entrance to the Underground City. With some reluctance, fully aware that I would be heading off in search of a place he had sworn did not exist, he swung his car around and drove me there.

He dumped me without ceremony in a swish business district and pulled off with a screech of tyres. I walked away from the wide road into a side alley, where the glass-sided buildings gave way to the patchy tiles and single-storey huts of a typical hutong. Melon-sellers pretended not to see me, and a tea vendor suddenly developed a great interest in his shoelaces. A mother grabbed two children close to her and scurried indoors, and I began to feel like the bad guy in a spaghetti western. Eventually, I found what I was looking for – a simple doorway in the street, flanked by a couple of small stone lions. I gingerly poked my head around the frame and came face to face with a young woman in army fatigues, who all but spat her noodles out in surprise.

'Hello,' I said. 'Can I see the Underground City?'

She looked around in panic and called downstairs for reinforcements.

'How did you find us?' she asked, setting down her noodles and standing almost to attention.

'There is,' I pointed out timidly, 'a sign outside in two languages.'

Two more women in camouflage arrived, and they immediately began interrogating me. Their questions were polite queries delivered with icy smiles. Where exactly had I come from? How had I even heard of the Underground City? When I demonstrated that their secret base had half a page to itself in the Lonely Planet guidebook, they seemed faintly crestfallen.

The first stirrings of the Underground City were humble enough – bomb shelters sunk into basements all across the city at the height of Cold War fears about nuclear Armageddon. The emperors might have been gone, but it only took the faintest whiff of paranoia in Chairman Mao for the whole city to be engaged with picks and shovels. Before long, news had drifted in from the Soviet Union of grander schemes – entire towns constructed inside mountains, designed to hold fast against atomic weapons.

Those first basement shelters were extended out and down, carved by the hands of tens of thousands of conscripted workers. Two stories beneath the streets, human labour scraped spaces in the rock for a hospital, a cinema and a military arsenal. Although scraps of archive footage show the shelters cluttered and crowded, with residents growing mushrooms and raising chickens in apocalyptic squalor, today the tunnels are white and bare. The occasional portrait of Mao or Cultural Revolution slogan adds a scrap of local colour, and antechambers behind half-hearted partitions still seem full of junk, like a Cold War jumble sale. My guide – a short, chirpy girl in camo-pattern clothes – accompanied me 'for my own safety', pointing out lesser tunnels devoid of electric light and helping me across places where flooding forced us to balance on precarious duckboards. She was friendly enough, but something about her demeanour made me neglect to mention I learned my Mandarin in Taiwan.

There is a romance to the Underground City, in the bizarre way that it is presented to the outside world. Thousands of Beijing residents formed the work gangs that carved out the tunnels – George H. Bush, in his account of his own visit to the tunnels, claims that 70% of the digging was done by women. They dug in fear for their very lives, under threat not just from foreign atomic weaponry but also from their own leaders, who swore them to the utmost secrecy. This stealthy attitude persists – the Underground City has become a well-known tourist attraction among foreigners, but has been kept menacingly quiet by Beijing locals, who are discouraged from visiting. As for those like me who brave the obstacles, a theme-park Cold War experience awaits – traditional Chinese inquisitiveness, which can often strike the Westerner as plain nosy, takes on an exotic, exciting sheen when doled out by women dressed as soldiers.

But that is part of its charm. The Underground City is a creation of innuendo – unmentioned and denied, allowed to flourish in the imagination. Rumours cling to it like weeds. Wide-eyed visitors whisper that its tunnels extend for hundreds of miles beneath the city, that it forms an empty space beneath the ground, like a negative Great Wall. Guides repeatedly claim that it stretches across 85 square kilometres, with at least one arm reaching out all the way to Beijing's airport, and another to the port city of Tianjin.

Those few Chinese who are prepared to discuss it at all

fall victim to their own country's media blackout. None are completely sure when it was built – it makes most sense for it to have been constructed in the 1950s or 1960s, but most seem convinced that it was dug in the 1970s. China and the Soviet Union had long been drifting apart, but disagreements over the nature of Communism were no longer matters for mere debate. Back in Moscow, Leonid Brezhnev made it clear that he was prepared to defend Moscow's brand of Communism by invading Communist states that dissented. Czechoslovakia and Hungary served as small but ominous examples. Beijing and Moscow risked turning into full-blown enemies. Chinese and Soviet troops clashed in 1969 over the border island of Zhenbao, and the septuagenarian Chairman Mao feared, with some justification, that open conflict might break out.

Except that is not quite true. The Zhenbao border skirmish was provoked by Mao himself, in one of several attempts to show the United States that he was no friend of the Soviet Union. At the time that many would have us believe that the tunnels were under construction, America was well and truly on a path to becoming China's friend. The only American invaders in Beijing were a startled team of ping-pong players, who were caught up in diplomatic intrigues when one member innocently suggested it might be nice to see China, leading to the team being swiftly whisked away on a surprise tourist trip. When the coast was declared clear, it was Richard Nixon who made the greatest gesture of all, descending upon China for a historic meeting that helped lure China back into the international community. Surely it was no time to be digging tunnels.

Were they even dug at all? The section on view to the public is impressive, but we only have the guides' word that it stretches across the entire city. They would say that, wouldn't they? Like the caves of Zhoukoudian, like the stones of the Great Wall, it is not the dank passageway itself that impresses but the prospect of thousands more like it, lacing the city in Cold War stealth. But I have not seen a map of all the tunnels. Nobody has. Could it be that the Underground City is not a physical feature at all, but an ideological one – a frightening vision of a state that will stop at nothing to preserve itself? Not for nothing, the bulk of the visitors who come to the Underground City are overseas Chinese – excitable tourists from a Taiwan still viewed by Beijing as a rogue province, ready to hear outrageous war stories about the Communist war machine. They come to be amazed by the fanaticism of their one-time enemies. And then they buy a skirt.

The Underground City's largest room, a meeting hall ten metres below street level, was leased to a Jiangxi silk company. Just when one's day cannot get any more surreal, one is surprised by a lecture on silkworm cultivation and invited to take part in the picking and preparation of silk from cocoons. It is an enlightening lecture, and all the more strange for taking place in a secret bunker.

But what if the Underground City is real? How many Beijing banks have vaults that lie precariously close to a tunnel network? How many apartment blocks have foundations undermined by secret dwellings for forgotten Party cadres? One need merely look at the Great Wall to see what China is capable of. Why *not* dig a city beneath the earth? Perhaps there is another reason for the Underground City's stealthy status – the government prefers not to reveal just how big it is. Or perhaps much of it has already been repurposed. Just as Londoners in the Blitz used Tube stations as bomb shelters, perhaps Beijing refashioned much of its underground network for use by subway trains. It is, perhaps, not a coincidence that whispered secrets about family members conscripted to dig the Underground City appear to coincide precisely with the construction of China's first subway in 1969. It has long been suspected, but never quite confirmed, that the immense speed with which Beijing acquired a dozen new subway lines in the twenty-first century relied, at least in part, on the ability of town planners to repurpose miles upon miles of secret tunnels. There are, however, several remnants of the Underground City that have been acknowledged, including a basement shopping centre in Yuetan, the huge underground ice rink beneath Ditan Park and, unsurprisingly, much of the tunnel system carved beneath the city by the Line 2 subway.

Opening in 1971, the Beijing subway was only one of many modern developments that heralded China's slow emergence from the hell of the Cultural Revolution. International flights returned in the early 1970s, along with telegraph and phone links to the outside world. A generation of angst at the United Nations was ended when the People's Republic of China took over the Chinese seat on the Security Council. The Nationalist Chinese of Taiwan were now diplomatic orphans, recognised by ever fewer states, losing their friends one by one and being forced to come up with increasingly intricate ways of describing themselves as independent without saying the word. It was not until the early 1980s that China itself was prepared to declare the Cultural Revolution a mistake and its instigators traitors.

Lord Macartney may have once expressed surprise at the close-quarter living arrangements of Old Beijing, but the Communist era saw residents packed even closer. Old Manchu mansions, outbuildings arranged around a central courtyard, were brutally repurposed to hold five, six, seven or more families. For much of the twentieth century, Beijing's hutong neighbourhoods became synonymous with socialist squalor, the central wells of old replaced with single toilet facilities to serve all the surrounding buildings. Already forced into each other's laps by small living quarters, Beijing residents were required to share what we might also optimistically call a 'bathroom' with over a dozen strangers.

Some, however, are more equal than others. The Party is still a major presence in Beijing. Go north of Tiananmen Square and walk the long straight road to the west of the Forbidden City, and the streets are hauntingly deserted. There are none of the traditional amenities – no roadside hawkers, photo shops, bistros or convenience stores. There are no beggars, no grannies selling postcards. Nobody is loitering, because anyone who does is moved swiftly along by the military police. This is where the political faithful live, as they did in Mao's day, clustered around the Zhongnanhai Park.

The Goddess of Democracy

There is still discord (some might say debate) within the Party. This comes not from the handful of vestigial democratic parties that simply rubber-stamp the decrees of the Communists. It comes from the people themselves. A state that owed so much of its origins to the 4 May Movement could not easily end all public protests, particularly when Communism was supposedly founded on the will of the people. Late in 1978, the first stirrings of protest were felt again at what became known as the Democracy Wall – an innocuous section of sports stadium brickwork that became a magnet for posters and poems outlining things that needed to be done. Before long, the Democracy Wall was relocated to a nearby park by government order, and protesters were later obliged to have their comments screened by the authorities first.

Other protests showed unsettling signs of the rebellions of the past. The city erupted in violence in May 1985, when the home team lost a soccer match against Hong Kong and thousands of hooligans poured out to vent their anger, somewhat ironically, against 'foreigners'. The unrest was met with a swift and tough crackdown on the offenders and a hurried government apology:

> Last night's incident is the worst of its kind in the history of sports in the People's Republic, and the most damaging to China's international image. This type of ignorant and brutish behaviour is quite out of keeping with the stature of our capital city.

The year 1989 saw the most famous political protest in modern Beijing, a chilling reminder to the outside world. It began, supposedly, with the death of Hu Yaobang, a relatively liberal politician who had been forced to resign over contemporary student protests and died soon after of natural causes. Some of his student supporters were soon in Tiananmen Square to show their support and were joined by older members of the workforce unhappy with recent price hikes. The Tiananmen Square protests thus began in confusion, with disaffected Chinese assembling in the square and demanding... *something*, although it seems difficult to see what. 'Democracy' seems to have been the buzzword – although the first stirrings of a free market were precisely what was causing the price hikes that had so angered some of the protesters in the first place.

Whatever this democracy was, it soon gained a new icon, courtesy of students at the Central Academy of Fine Arts who assembled the famous Goddess of Democracy, a ten-metre statue of styrofoam and papier-mâché supported on a metal frame, in just four days. Its size was carefully calculated for extreme visibility, since decades of propaganda had made the students amateur experts: if the army smashed down the statue, as they eventually did, it would be a powerful political statement in its own right. Until that moment, the Goddess was carefully placed in the square, facing the giant image of Mao himself on the Gate of Heavenly Peace, defiantly brandishing a flaming torch.

By May 1989, hundreds of protesters were camped out in Tiananmen Square, and all attempts to move them had failed. Sympathetic government officials had pleaded with them not to make a spectacle, with voices that became all the more strident as several hundred protesters resolved to go on hunger strike. Levels of government embarrassment climbed steadily as the date approached for a state visit by the Soviet leader, Mikhail Gorbachev. Keen to avoid an encounter between a Russian reformer and student radicals, the Chinese government routed Gorbachev's motorcade through a series of outrageous detours to avoid Beijing's main thoroughfare.

With Gorbachev's departure, the gloves were off. At 10:30 p.m. on 3 June, the People's Liberation Army (PLA) was sent in to clear the square. The use of the military to police a civilian disturbance ended in tragedy, an event remembered today as the Tiananmen Square Massacre. Protesters were forcibly removed from the square and from their enclave to the west of it.

This would have placed them right outside the Party residences in Zhongnan Park. Precise details, however, are hard to come by. Those who watched the whole thing on television were initially led to believe that thousands of people had died. These numbers seem to be based upon vague guesses by harassed medical personnel and shocked foreign reporters at the scene, and may have confused casualties with fatalities. Not that a single death was justified, but in the years since the massacre it has been difficult to find a list of the dead that climbs above 200. The trauma of the Tiananmen Square Massacre had far-reaching effects. Liberals like Zhao Ziyang were drummed out of office, blamed for the very unrest that he had tried to dissuade. Martial law stayed in force until 1990 and might have been upheld for longer if it were not for Beijing's desire to normalise its appearance to the outside world. The economic reforms that some protesters demanded more of, and others wanted to stop for good, were briefly delayed in the aftermath, but were soon reinstated in China's inexorable drive towards a freer market. In the years since the PLA smashed the fragile Goddess of Democracy into pieces, much stronger and more enduring replicas of the statue have sprung up in overseas Chinese communities – most notably on the western seaboard of North America, where they continue to stir controversy between supporters and opponents of the Communist regime.

In the hours leading up to the attack, there was a debate among the protesters as to how they should meet it. Many were keen to leave the square peacefully, although as on 4 May seventy years earlier a militant element was determined to fight back. To hear the army's version of events, it was these militants, armed with petrol bombs, who fought back against the PLA. There were military casualties, too, in the Tiananmen Square Massacre, eliciting considerably less sympathy from the international community.

One soldier was faced with an intense diplomatic situation when the path of his tank was blocked by a lone figure. The unidentified man clutching two carrier bags who faced down an entire tank column became Beijing's most famous resident. In an iconic moment of the twentieth century, the unknown rebel harangued the driver of the lead tank about his mission, until passers-by wisely dragged him out of harm's way. His precise identity and his ultimate fate remain one of the mysteries of Beijing history.

Far away in Chengdu, someone remembered the words of Lu Xun from 1926 and wrote them on a wall: 'All blood debts must be repaid in kind.'

Twelve years after tanks rolled across Tiananmen Square, the International Olympic Committee (IOC) announced that Beijing would become the centre of the world once more: in August 2008, the city would play host to the Olympic Games.

8

Beijing Welcomes You: 1989–2008

Jianguomen, the 'Gate of Building the Nation', is long gone, but still lends its name to the street that once went through it and an intersection where it once stood. Its 'inner' and 'outer' stretches are divided by a giant broken-arched rainbow, its multiple colours illuminated at night. Local expats usually call it the Big Gay Rainbow, associating it with Gilbert Baker's globally recognised pride flag celebrating diversity in the LGBT community. That, however, has got nothing to do with it.

The rainbow on Jianguomen and a twin arch on the far side of the city were intended to represent something very different – the 'return' of Hong Kong to Chinese sovereignty in 1997. The wording is deliberate; what was known as the 'handover' in Anglophone media, regarded by many with caution and melancholy, was a moment of great jubilation throughout much of the Chinese community, even in non-Communist Taiwan. For China and the Chinese, 1997 was a watershed in China's recovery from a century of humiliation, and an important point on the road to greatness. The twenty-first century, thought by many to be China's prospective new golden age, was only a few years away, and the rainbow marks its advent. For the China-watcher, it is a little ironic, and perhaps fitting, that hardly

anyone who passes the big, glowing, multi-coloured instal-
lation knows what it actually represents.

The handover was only one of China's improvements on
the road to modernisation and globalisation. The hosting
of the Olympic Games was another. Its legacy can be seen
in concrete form in the north of the city, in the architecture of the Olympic village, and in ongoing attempts by
the authorities to find some way of using the facilities for
posterity.

Beijing's involvement with the Olympics is surprisingly
recent. China only participated in the games on four occasions before 1956, the period of the first Five-Year Plan, and
had been totally absent thereafter until 1984. The era of the
Cultural Revolution killed more than just education and
development; it even killed sport.

The achievement of actually hosting the games was an
incredible learning curve – a superhuman effort, all the
more daunting considering the low ebb of international
opinion in the wake of the Tiananmen Square Massacre.
Planning began in February 1999, when President Jiang
Zemin addressed a national conference in Beijing on 'Pro-
moting the World's Understanding of China'. The President's inaugural speech emphasised the need to 'teach the
world' about China; amid suggestions that China might
also have something to learn from the world in return, he
urged his people to educate the rest of the world about
China's own history.

Beijing had hosted the Asian Games in 1990, pouring
US$300 million into new building programmes for the
expected guests. Some of the initiatives were more cosmetic

– the plastering over of bullet holes at the edges of Tiananmen Square and the repaving of avenues to remove the telltale tank tracks gouged in the road.

Even so, China would not be forgiven so easily. Representatives of the IOC arrived in 1993 to discuss Beijing's bid to host the Olympics in 2000 and were regaled with documentaries about China's rich cultural heritage, as well as the bizarre promise by Beijing's mayor that all the delegates would be immortalised in a plaque on the Great Wall, if they only agreed. Ironically, part of the Chinese pitch for the games rested on totalitarian guarantees of an obedient population, assuring the IOC that there would be no protests or trouble. In a strange reversal of the drab Mao era, schoolchildren were instructed to dress in brightly coloured clothes, and were bussed in to Tiananmen Square by the thousand. Meanwhile, behind the scenes, coal-burning heaters and smoky factories were shut down for the duration of the IOC's visit; in order to ensure clear blue skies over the city, many citizens were deprived of hot water and sent home from industrial jobs.

The Beijing 2000 bid was an impressive effort, all the more remarkable considering how swiftly the Chinese had to learn to play the international game. But Beijing's cosmopolitan status was still doubtful, with relatively few international flights and a population lacking in English skills. The smog-busting ruse had also failed – the delegates thought that environmental protection in Beijing was still substandard. Crucially for a global sporting event that relied on the attention of the world, Beijing's telecommunications were deemed not up to global standards.

Yet none of these problems was a deal-breaker – there was still a chance that the Beijing bid might be successful if the organisers were able to give the appropriate assurances. According to one rumour, the final straw, tipping the decision in favour of Sydney by just two votes, was an ill-advised moment of old-school Party bluster, when a Chinese official suggested that China would not bother with future Olympic games if it failed to win the 2000 bid. It was exactly the wrong thing to say to the IOC. The Olympics' own mission statement emphasised international understanding, global cooperation and competition in friendly rivalry; it was not about to cave to retaliatory threats or pre-emptive sulking.

The Fiftieth Anniversary

The failure of the 2000 bid clearly hurt the Beijing committee, which had accomplished amazing things, even if they were ultimately unsuccessful. In the aftermath, Beijing temporarily retreated into itself, announcing a Five-Year Plan of renewal and renovation, which improved conditions in the city for the fiftieth anniversary celebration of the founding of the People's Republic – an aim that would please the Party faithful without the loss of face that a second bid on the international stage might have occasioned.

Crucially, the city's government finally admitted in February 1998 that Beijing suffered from some of the worst air pollution in the world, with the ever-present dusty winds from the western deserts augmented by coal-based pollution and the usual smog of an industrial centre with a growing population of automobiles. New traffic laws denuded the streets of some of the worst smoke-belching vehicles but also reduced the number of bicycle-only lanes in what had once been a city where pedals and the pedicab were the default forms of transportation.

Beijing residents were encouraged to change not just their city but also themselves, in a programme to teach them better manners – less spitting in the street (punished, Singapore-style, by a US$6 fine), improved hygiene and a better sense of personal space. The eleventh day of each month in the year preceding the Olympics became Queuing Day, in which locals could receive awards for displaying a more internationally acceptable grasp of the importance of standing in an orderly line and not cutting in. A nine-point pledge appeared on billboards all over the city, demanding that 'civilised residents' abide by maxims of acceptable behaviour. Some, such as an admonition to practise family planning, were old-school Chinese Communist slogans. Others, such as the commandment to 'love science and respect teachers' were powerful about-faces from the Mao-era contempt for learning. Still more, such as a demand to 'be polite to guests', seemed aimed at preparing Beijing citizenry for an influx of thousands of Olympic visitors. A unit of 'English police' – two scholars, one Chinese and one English – was formed and tasked with hunting down bad spelling and grammar in Beijing signs in order to avoid embarrassing howlers. There was even a phone number set up for people to report errors in public signage, although the journalist Pallavi Aiyar reported calling it one day, only to discover that the lady at the other end didn't speak English.

Beijing citizens were expected to learn English, with local workers being encouraged to take lessons, and useful phrases cropping up in new sections of newspapers. In particular, Beijing taxi drivers were singled out as the likely front line of many foreign visitors' interactions with China, since it was widely understood that foreigners would leap upon the chance to be chauffeur-driven around town for an average cost of US$2 a trip. Beijing cab drivers had to hand out numbered receipts, and most appear to have been well drilled in putting the customer first.

The Demolition Derby

Jasper Becker, in *The City of Heavenly Tranquillity*, suggests that the death knell for old Beijing was sounded much earlier, in 1982, when the government made a drastic change to the law and constitution. Urban land was reassigned to the ownership of the state, matching similar transfers in the countryside and turning every Chinese homeowner into a mere tenant. At any point, with only minimal warning, the authorities could snatch land back from its occupiers and were only obliged to compensate them for the loss of the building materials on the site.

With residents discouraged from spending their own money on renovating a building that could be taken away from them at any moment, a decade of decay set in. A second punch landed in 1992, when authorities claiming to be 'surprised' by tumbledown districts introduced new legislation that allowed for the 'reform of dangerous residential buildings'.

'In this way,' writes Becker, 'a local government could

decide to level an entire neighbourhood whenever it saw fit, simply by declaring it a slum.' Throughout the 1990s and the 2000s, investors with the right connections were able to requisition whole city blocks – which was handy for Olympic facilities and, in the years since, for the sudden mushrooming of skyscrapers, shopping malls and other large-scale developments.

One of the most severe casualties of Beijing's remodelling was the old hutong lifestyle. Converting nineteenth-century homes into twentieth-century hovels, a temporary measure that long since outgrew its usefulness, was no longer desirable – not merely for matters of hygiene and living standards, but for simple economies of space. Hutong buildings rarely climbed above a single storey, whereas modern China favours huge tower blocks stacking residents on top of one another. Ousted residents were either relocated to satellite towns or offered apartments in the towers that sat on the sites of their former houses. Few, however, could resist the temptation to cash in the increased value, selling their windfall residences before the paint was dry, effectively exiling themselves from the city that was once their home.

Another watershed moment occurred when planning permission was granted for Li Ka-shing, the richest man in Hong Kong, to build Oriental Plaza, a multi-use mall and residential complex in Wangfujing that rode roughshod over the careful limits on building near the Forbidden City. Li's grand project was the subject of multiple arguments and setbacks, not least because it was five times taller than previous zoning restrictions allowed, leading to accusations that planning officials had been bribed to give in to his demands. While building was underway, there was an inevitable case of rescue archaeology, as workers uncovered the remains of a prehistoric campsite. In a rare example of heritage awareness, this was incorporated into the site, and you can still drop in on the Wangfujing Paleolithic Museum in the basement of the shopping mall. It is, in fact, probably the only reason to go there unless you are suddenly taken over with a desperate desire to buy some Bose speakers or a Hugo Boss tie. Completed in 2004, Oriental Plaza has also become something of an icon of the precarious nature of China's modern investment boom. It cost Li 20 billion yuan to build but, as is usual with all commercial buildings in China, Li only had a fifty-year lease on the land, ten years of which had already elapsed during the site's construction. Despite all the bluster and consumption, critics noted that his chances of getting anything more than a modest return on his investment were minimal.

More reforms were part of a 'Toilet Revolution', as Beijing locals were instructed in suitable behaviour. Decades of hutong life had left Beijing residents with little sense of privacy, and many foreign visitors returned with shocking horror stories of dirty holes in the ground and communal shit-pits. China gained its own 'ideal toilet' exhibition, designed to introduce the no-nonsense locals to the concept of closing a stall door – and, indeed, to the existence of stalls and stall doors in the first place.

The government began hunting down Beijing's growing underclass of peasants and vagrants from other parts of China, lured by capitalist-inspired dreams of finding their fortune and often left to subsist in off-the-grid shanty towns and overpopulated flophouses. In September 1999, just one month before the fiftieth anniversary of the People's Republic, officials initiated a purge of the Three Withouts: those without papers, those without residence permits and those without a legitimate and permanent income. Thousands of beggars and tramps were rounded up, while a separate modernisation programme, using the 1992 law as a hammer, demolished 2.6 million square metres of 'illegal structures' – lean-tos, huts and sheds used as accommodation by the rural poor. A common symbol on Beijing walls was the character '*chai*' – a hand holding an axe – marking any building for destruction, making it an empty-space-in-waiting. In a moment of foolhardy architectural protest, some new buildings constructed as part of the renewal protest also gained a *chai* graffito, scrawled on their walls by unknown parties who disapproved of the speed and nature of change.

The area around the Forbidden City was beautified with a wrecking ball, through the demolition of hundreds of Qing-dynasty mansions now dilapidated by decades of communal occupation – today, of all the noble dwellings in the area, only Prince Gong's is still standing and open to the public. The period created a huge discrepancy between wealth and wages, the big stereotype being the taxi driver on £12,000 a year who received a huge sum in compensation for his inner-city hovel and didn't know what to do with the money. This, in turn, fuelled a huge number of twentieth-century Chinese stock-market gambles, foreign travel and even overseas education.

Further out of the centre, officials disbanded and discouraged street markets, leading to a brief-but-telling city-wide shortage of fresh fruit and vegetables. There was also a minor controversy over the demolition of Xinjiang Alley – a street that had achieved a gourmet reputation with expats and students for its halal Uyghur cuisine. Despite grumblings from foreigners in Beijing, Xinjiang Alley was wiped off the face of the earth in February 1999 – many of the establishments had been built on public land without permits and hence stood little chance of resisting the demolition order.

Despite the controversies over the approach of the fiftieth anniversary celebrations, they also served to prove how foreign attention could lead to local reforms for the better. The upheavals were unwelcome, even when undertaken in the name of Communism and not the Olympics, but they also led to government initiatives to sweeten the pill with 'good news' programmes. Seemingly in an attempt to counterbalance complaints, people in the rest of China were told that social security payouts were to be increased and civil servants would receive a 30% pay rise, backdated for several months. But to many outside observers the 1999 anniversary celebrations were another sham, with the obligatory military pageant and its counterproductive security measures that forced people who lived on the route of the parade to keep their windows shuttered throughout.

In February 2001, Beijing was prepared to try again to impress the IOC, with the arrival of an inspection team to see how the city had developed. To local residents, it was a repeat of the previous attempt, with a mass mobilisation of street-sweepers and painters before the IOC's arrival and a round-up of the usual suspects. This time, the plan worked, and the IOC announced on 13 July 2001 that the Olympics in 2008 would take place in Beijing.

More than a decade after the 2008 Olympics, their paraphernalia can still be found in junk shops and the more ramshackle shopping centres. The city had not one but five Olympic mascots, in what the Olympic adverts claimed to be a 'message of friendship and peace', which really seem to be an acknowledgement of the only force more powerful than realpolitik: marketing. The cartoonish Olympic mascots were a menagerie of Chinese creatures, conceived as 'collectable' for all those capitalist visitors, whose children should pester them to bring back not just one cuddly toy or action figure or key chain, but five. The mascots were a colour-coded team; traditionalists might hope to link them to the Chinese elements, but their conception owes more to branded Japanese team-shows like *Power Rangers*, their nominal leader a fiery personification of the Olympic flame. Foreign visitors were exhorted to collect the entire set as if they were Pokémon or some other consumerist craze, from the ubiquitous panda and the predictable fish (for water sports) to a politically sensitive Tibetan antelope. The fifth mascot character was a spirit of the air, appearing on logos for such pursuits as badminton and fencing. As a bird totem, she was a swallow, personification of the ancient Land of Swallows and a symbol of Beijing's long-term poetic associations.

The mascots' names – Bei-bei, Jing-jing, Huang-huang, Ying-ying and Ni-ni – also formed a slogan, *Beijing huangying ni* ('Beijing Welcomes You'), which in turn formed the chorus of a ridiculously opulent pop video to promote the games, crammed with Chinese celebrities including Jackie Chan himself belting out the chorus from the Great Wall. The lyrics, which come across somewhat more clunkily in English than they do in Chinese, proclaim that the city welcomes all comers as honoured guests, that a big door is always open, and something about how miracles are the reward of courage.

My Own Beijing

This is, quite literally, where I came in, as my family obligations in China suddenly turned me from a tourist into a resident. In the early twenty-first century, I was catapulted into Chinese street life in an unexpected fashion, left to while away the days with my infant son while my former wife did whatever it was that she did at the People's University. Looking back over my diaries of several years in China, it's clear just how frantic the pace of change really was. Retreating from the shopping malls, I roamed some of the last of Beijing's hutongs, only to lament that they, too, were undergoing rapid transformation. A few were rescued in some form of heritage tourism, transformed into hipster enclaves – coffee shops and vinyl records, teahouses and music bars. More recently – though, unfortunately, tardily – the Chinese authorities have come to recognise the heritage value of the hutongs, leading to several becoming protected areas. While this has allowed a few nests of blue-collar workers to live close to the toilets they scrub and the shops they staff, in most cases it has led to soaring gentrification; Rupert Murdoch and his then-wife Wendi Deng supposedly paid millions for a *siheyuan* house within spitting distance of the Forbidden City. Perhaps they hoped it would be handy for the buses.

The last time I had been in Beijing, there had been only two subway lines. Now they were sprawling all over the city, with adverts flashing out on the tunnel walls in laser, timed to change with the speed of the carriage so that the pictures appeared to move. You would think you were facing featureless black walls, and then suddenly a floating princess with a sword would leap at you out of the darkness and try to sell you tea.

Some areas had enjoyed unexpected booms. Houhai, the lake area around what was once the inland terminus for the Grand Canal, is one of the most well-preserved of the hipster hutongs, retaining both old-world residential charm and new-age boutiques. It was once a sleepy district, only truly gaining its current nightlife and bustle since the SARS epidemic of 2003, when locals began to favour its outdoor tables and lakeside breezes over the close quarters of Sanlitun bars.

Older guidebooks, in fact, make Sanlitun sound like some sort of party paradise, as indeed it may have been back in the days when it catered to lonely embassy expats and the edgier among China's youth; it was supposedly the site of Beijing's first-ever Western-style bar, an unlikely claim considering the number of foreign hotels in the old Legation Quarter. While it still has dozens of little tourist-trappy drinking joints and cafés, the expansion of the city in the last decade has largely diluted much of what made it different. Sure enough, it has shopping malls all around and boasts the 'world's largest Adidas store' but, to me at least, it looks like much of the rest of Beijing. The open-air appeal of Houhai post-SARS was one more nail in Sanlitun's coffin... until the next round of rejuvenations.

Other hutongs were bulldozed to make way for towering shopping centres, but these, too, endured an evolutionary decline. They would start off packed with big-name franchises, shiny outposts for L'Occitane and Hugo Boss, but these would fade, migrating to newer, shinier malls, ceding the space to local products and pop-up markets. Within a couple of years, there would be a nylon tracksuit shop where there had once been a Tommy Hilfiger. The sole exception was in the children's sector, which experienced a boom as the Party's 'one-child policy' was relaxed and then suspended. Suddenly, children were the new lucrative investment area: clothing, prams and paraphernalia, and indoor playgrounds took over floor space in even the most second-rate malls.

Beijing's museum count took a sudden, exponential uptick during the approach of the 2008 Olympics, when the city government earmarked millions of yuan for the development of institutions commemorating every conceivable aspect of city life. In some cases, this led to the welcome restoration of derelict sites such as the Eunuch Culture Museum, or quirky exercises like the Tap Water Museum and other celebrations of old Beijing.

'Old Beijing', however, is a loaded term. Take, as a case in point, Dazhalan ('the great stockade'), usually garbled in local dialect as Dashilar. This street of shops, theatres and silk merchants judiciously preserves the flavour of the late Qing dynasty, when its location just outside the imperial enclave made it a flourishing trading post and arts community. 'Today we went into the Chinese City,' wrote Ellen LaMotte in 1916, 'and visited a native department store. At the best speed of our rickshaw boys we passed out of the [Qianmen], the principal gate, and once beyond the towering, embattled wall that separates the Chinese from the Tartar city, we lost ourselves in the maze of narrow, winding streets that open on all sides from the main road.'

She went to Dazhalan. There, a century later, you can still find Yueshengzhai, a butcher's shop founded in 1830 (originally to sell leftover meat from sacrifices and divinations); Tianhuizhai, Beijing's last surviving purveyor of snuff; and the Daguanlou, the very first cinema in Beijing, dating back to 1905. There's the Neiliansheng shoe shop (founded 1853) and, guarded by stone *qilin* unicorns, the Tongrentang medicine shop (established 1669 and moved to this spot in 1702) and the Duyichu dumpling restaurant (founded 1738), conferred with its name by its most famous client, the Qianlong Emperor. A street of more modern hawkers, selling the usual Little Red Books and furry hats, stretches north. Blink and you'll miss it, but a tiny alleyway leading away from this point is Qianshi Hutong. The former site of several silversmiths, it is accessed via the narrowest alleyway in Beijing, in order to hamper the escape of any potential thieves. At its narrowest point, it is only 40 centimetres wide.

While such curios attract many Chinese visitors, Dazhalan's main draw for foreign tourists is in its fabric and clothing stores. The most famous is Ruifuxiang, founded in 1893 and famed today as the supplier for the red silk used in the Communist flag that was first raised on the proclamation of independence. I love Dazhalan – I spent many happy days there haggling over silk and what passed for antiques, and dragging visitors through its bustling side streets. In later years, I found myself sniffily observing that it was going to the dogs, that there were too many fast-food franchises, that it really didn't need a sanitised concourse with a Tissot watch shop and a Madame Tussauds. The final straw for me was the bulldozing of a nearby hutong to make way for a Harrods branch selling British tea and Paddington bears.

But Dazhalan 'never was what it was'. Older hands, in China long before me, decried it from the outset as a sanitised, knowingly performative rendition of old Beijing. Certainly, its olde-worlde charm has been very carefully managed; it was one of the first places in Beijing to embrace a sense of commodified heritage, instead of desperately demolishing everything old in favour of anything new. Both Michael Meyer and Harriet Evans, in their respective books *The Last Days of Old Beijing* and *Beijing From Below,* independently treat Dazhalan as an epitome of Beijing's pell-mell rush to turn itself into a theme park of its own history at the expense of the real people who live in it.

Lamenting the decline of Dazhalan to a friend, I was told to seek out Nanluogu Xiang, a similar district north of the Forbidden City. For a while, I found there an echo of the way things once were. Around the Drum and Bell Tower districts, formerly squalid housing had been transformed into organic coffee shops, boutique restaurants and vinyl jazz emporia riddled with cocktail bars, trendily 'Taiwanese' ice cream parlours, and the unforgettable sight of the Plastered T-Shirts shopfront with its iconic, profane green llama in the window. I found it rather fun: a handy shopping area in which to pick up that all-important vampire costume, transforming model robot and/or bobble hat with cat ears. While it may not have been redolent of the Ming dynasty, it was certainly a vibrant part of contemporary Beijing life, even for locals – until, one day, it was turned into rubble without warning. I popped back a few months later to see what had become of it, and it now boasted a Starbucks.

A security guard came out to stare at me.

'What happened?' I asked.

'Progress,' he beamed.

9

Great Prosperity: 2008–2022

The train from Beijing West catapults you to the airport at 146 kilometres per hour. You find Wi-Fi at your seat, videos telling you how great the airport is, and a security guard in every carriage – just in case the multiple cameras aren't watchful enough. And when you get out at the terminal, you are confronted by a giant slogan floating in mid-air: 'The motherland is strong and the nation is rejuvenated – great prosperity'. But, as you approach, the huge characters are revealed as something else. They are composed of hundreds upon hundreds of little origami swans, strung up in praise of the Party and the people.

Daxing ('great prosperity') Airport was an exercise in one-upmanship and record-breaking. As if Beijing Capital Airport was not enough – and it apparently wasn't – the week before the celebration of the seventieth anniversary of the People's Republic in 2019 saw the opening of an even bigger monument to China's modernity. Daxing will ultimately have 'at least' eight runways – and specialised military ones are not included in the official count. With the hyper-qualification common to Chinese bragging, it has the largest *single-building* air terminal, and a *theoretical* capacity to handle 150 million passengers a year, which, *if used*, would make it the busiest airport in the world.

Publicists were even eager to report its first big award in 2020: 'Best Airport by Hygiene Measures', according to Airports Council International.

Through no fault of its designers and managers, Daxing was opened in September 2019, just a couple of months before people in a Wuhan fish market started coming down with weird flu-like symptoms, the first signs of the global COVID-19 pandemic. International travel was shut down for months, all Chinese tourist visas were cancelled and even business travellers were doomed to a two-week quarantine on arrival. Daxing's first two years of operation saw a greatly reduced number of passengers, a mere trickle of international flyers ready to gawp at the soaring starfish-shaped terminal or ride the new bullet train into the city centre. You bet it had good hygiene measures, starting with having almost nobody to clean up after; some of the first travellers to arrive marvelled at the earnest desire of the staff to look busy.

Daxing effectively increased the size of Beijing once more. The new airport was 46 kilometres south of Tiananmen Square but was bolted firmly into the ever-growing metro system. Some 20,000 local villagers were evicted from their homes to make space for the airport, and further relocations are expected once full operations ramp up the noise pollution. For the local inhabitants, generous offers of moving grants belied the disruption caused by the loss of a way of life. One farmer told the press that, while he was grateful for his compensation and his new apartment in town, 'You don't have land to grow on. And you have to figure out a new life.' What had once been open farmland was now dragged into the orbit of the capital city and, with it, its history. Workmen on the site inevitably uncovered archaeological remains – some 200 graves dating back to the Qing era, clustered together in such a fashion as to suggest that they represented the family cemetery of a particular lineage or clan.

Daxing's design, for which it is widely praised as one of the most beautiful airports in the world, also offers a glimpse of Beijing's digitally ingested, surveillance-conscious future. For passengers' supposed convenience, 76% of luggage check-ins are self-service, tracked through RFID chips visible on apps, so that when you realise you've put your suitcase on the wrong conveyor belt, you will presumably be able to watch in horror on your iPhone in real time as it is loaded on a flight to Brazil. Even if *you* get lost, the airport will not lose track of you, since many of its facilities require submission to facial recognition software.

In the *New York Times*, Ian Johnson observed that the pressure to build Daxing had less to do with airport logistics and more to do with infrastructure issues behind the scenes. It was possible, he argued, for the pre-existing Capital Airport to handle much of the increased passenger load of the 2020s, were it not hobbled by the Chinese air force, which zoned off so much of Chinese airspace for exclusive military use that civilian aircraft were stuck in tiny, narrow slots mid-air. It was this invisible congestion, he claimed, that caused so many flight delays in China and crammed so many passengers into limited windows for their flights.

He may have a point, although there are plenty of other

issues plaguing Chinese air travel, including air pollution around Beijing so thick that aerial visibility drops below acceptable levels and rainstorms that can put runways out of action for hours. Not to mention the relative ease, comfort and reliability of high-speed rail in China: once you factor in the time spent tramping to and from the airport, getting through check-in and waiting for a flight (which, in my experience, is going to be delayed half the time anyway), you might as well let the train take the strain.

One such train now shoots with impressive speed from Beijing North station to Zhangjiakou in just 47 minutes, a sufficiently short time to obscure the fact that, until Beijing won the bid to stage the 2022 Winter Olympics, the old-style rail journey took over three hours. Much has been made of the fact that Beijing will go down in history as the first city to host both the Summer and Winter Olympic games, although that's not quite the whole truth. While the Bird's Nest – the Beijing National Stadium – is indeed the first location to stage opening and closing ceremonies for both events, much of the winter sports competitions taking place in 'Beijing' are actually located in Yanqing, which is 90 kilometres away, and Zhangjiakou, which, despite being the site of 'Beijing's' cross-country skiing, ski-jumping, biathlon and snowboarding events, is actually 220 kilometres out of town.

And so it is that Zhangjiakou, a strategically important mountain pass as far away from Tiananmen Square as New York is from Washington, is the latest satellite community to be incorporated into the history of Beijing. There has been a bit of careful media massaging of this fact, most obviously in the recent overuse of Zhangjiakou's nickname, the Northern Gate of Beijing, which makes it sound like it is on the edge of the suburbs and not up near the Inner Mongolian border. In fact, its former name, Kalgan, does indeed mean 'gate' in Mongol, but refers to the nearby opening in the Great Wall, marking the edge of pre-modern China.

At least the Winter Olympics were good news for the Bird's Nest stadium, which, despite its impressive appearance and iconic status, has struggled to pay its way in the years since 2008 – costing US$11 million a year to simply maintain, and leading to a number of hare-brained schemes to attract customers when it is not hosting pop stars or lesser sporting events, such as its annual conversion into a ski resort with artificial snow from January to February. The fact that it can be repurposed and used as a venue for the Olympics a second time is something of a thrifty coup for the Chinese state and helps explain how the Winter Olympics were brought in at a tenth of the budget of their Summer forerunners.

The City and the City

Where does it all end? In 2014, the writer Hao Jingfang published a novelette that would go on to win the international Hugo Award for science fiction – only the second Chinese work ever to do so. It was called *Folding Beijing*, and it imagined life in the city if it continued to grow at its dizzying, relentless pace. Looking ahead, Hao imagined a Seventh Ring Road, inflation pushing up the price of fresh fruit tenfold, terrible pollution and a drastic solution to the population problem. Hao's Beijing now involved three separate classes occupying the same space, hot-bedding between their allotted times to leave their homes. Five million lucky souls lived in the First Space, enjoying daylight hours and clean public amenities. From six in the evening until ten at night, the city belonged to the 25 million inhabitants of Second Space, mostly shift workers supplying the needs of the upper class, their homes and offices folding out of the ground to occupy the city for the evening. At 10 p.m., even the Second Spacers fold away, leaving the city in the hands of 50 million Third Spacers until dawn – the cleaners, garbage men and menial labourers, many of them lacking the correct paperwork or any prospects.

Beyond the numbers, Hao's dystopia bears a strong relationship to the city as it already is. In the year after Hao wrote *Folding Beijing*, the transport authority ended the two-*kuai* (20p) flat-fee cost of tickets on the Beijing subway in recognition of the fact that journey lengths could now stretch for dozens of kilometres. The decision was met with howls of protest from locals, not the least because everybody needed to work out the varying prices to each destination. For me, it also ruined one of the best lines in Mark Griffith's 2013 parody rap song 'Beijing State of Mind':

Hop onto the subway, the smell it ain't so lovely
But at just two *kuai* I don't mind getting cuddly.

Hao Jingfang's Seventh Ring Road became a reality in 2018, only four years after she wrote of it. Indeed, local slang already refers to Highway 112, which circles Beijing at a radius of 200 kilometres, as the city's de facto Eighth Ring

Road. And while government officials may gripe and kvetch about unregistered migrants, Beijing, like other Chinese cities, already has a huge underclass of maids, cleaners and labourers, many of them former farm folk rebranded as urban workers at the same time as they were bussed off their fields to their new city apartments. Hao regarded the differing levels of access to resources as being the signs of a bifurcation not merely of classes but practically of races, as if the people of Beijing were stratifying themselves into prototypes of H. G. Wells' Eloi and Morlocks. And it's true that the Beijing experience can be very different depending on where you end up.

Dispatched to a hotel in the north-east of the city to meet up with a film crew for a documentary project, I found myself in an odd enclave that catered to expats. Suspended in the no-man's-land between the airport and the city were leafy suburbs and English-language kindergartens, a general store that sold foreign snacks and junk food, and a restaurant where the waitresses swiftly scurried off to get the *other* menu when I ordered in Chinese. The items on the new one were half the previous price.

'I'm sorry,' said the waitress. 'We thought you were one of Them.'

Not even the expat experience is the same all over Beijing. On the outskirts of Ritan Park, the signage is all in Cyrillic, and the pedicab drivers all call out to me in Russian, acknowledging that this little piece of Beijing – just a couple of streets wide – is really a Little Moscow. And the last of the hutongs remain run-down and squalid, inexplicably passed over in the rush to modernise. I imagine fervid politicking behind the scenes, possibly even within the same family, as an aged granny demands to live the way she has for decades, her taxi-driving son wishes for a shopping mall to buy the family out, and her starry-eyed granddaughter dreams of retaining the hutong buildings but turning them into an organic bakery – or a textile collective, or some other bijou distraction for tourists.

Think-tanks suggest that 2030 is the year when everything will change, when China's population will finally plateau, and when green initiatives will start to bear fruit. The Beijing Municipal Commission for City Planning and Land Resources Management wants to increase the tree coverage in the streets and parks to 45% of the city by 2030, hoping in turn that this will help reduce the particulate content of the city's notorious smog. The ever-expanding subway network, already at 1,000 kilometres in length, is part of an initiative to reduce cars on the streets, as is a plan to make 12.6% of city commutes bicycle-based by 2030. By then, Beijing will be bigger but have fewer buildings as more sites are supposedly greened.

But how much bigger? Bigger than even Hao Jingfang imagined, with the proposal of the Beijing-Tianjin-Hebei Integration Plan, or Jing-Jin-Ji for short, conflating Beijing with the nearby coastal metropolis of Tianjin and with much of the land in the surrounding Hebei province. Roughly coinciding with the span of Highway 112, the plan would create a conurbation with a population of 100 million over 200,000 square kilometres, from Zhangjiakou in the hills to Tianjin on the coast, covering a region that already accounts for 10% of China's GDP. To put that in perspective, it would create a 'city' within China that is larger than each of the *nations* of Uganda and Belarus, and not all that much smaller than Great Britain. Supposedly, Beijing is capping its permanent population at 23 million, but the Jing-Jin-Ji project makes it clear that this cap will become a mere number on a chart as areas are rezoned and redefined. The long-term China-sceptic will immediately start to wonder about that '45% green' statistic, bearing in mind that 'Beijing' itself may be rezoned to incorporate land that is (at least momentarily) open countryside, thereby ticking that quota box shortly before a new phase of rebuilding begins. This requires more rail, more roads and, of course, more airports: Jing-Jin-Ji is not some new fantasy but an idea that has been sitting on the government's Five-Year Plans since 2011. Daxing Airport has been part of it all along.

Jing-Jin-Ji is only one of a number of grand megaprojects occupying Chinese investors in the 2020s. In fact, one might even say it is a response or counterpart to at least two others: the Great Bay project that is assimilating Hong Kong, Macao and Guangzhou in the South, and the Yangtze Delta sprawl, destined to unite Shanghai, Ningbo and points nearby. These 'mega-city regions' are liable to form power blocs in future government wrangles, jockeying for funding and investment as city 'mayors' wield a power and influence more befitting ancient kings. Maybe someone could make a modest proposal: that the Jing-Jin-Ji megalopolis be renamed Yanjing, since it would encompass much of the territory of the old Land of Swallows.

Modern Ghosts

The 2008 and 2022 Olympics were programmes of wide-scale renovation for Beijing, easily equivalent to the sweeping transformations of Khubilai Khan or the Yongle Emperor. Every nation that holds the Olympics ends up asking itself the same questions: Are we really helping our own people? Will this really improve our infrastructure? Or in ten years will there be hungry beggars huddling for shelter in the shell of an empty stadium? Beijing has seen many Five-Year Plans and grand schemes; it has been razed to the ground on numerous occasions. Will this latest project bring true good, or will it create more discord than it quells, instilling the local poor with grand expectations and a sense of entitlement to something that the future may not be able to provide?

It used to be that as the tourist reached the final approach to the Great Wall at Simatai, a crowd of hawkers waited hungrily. With little to do but loiter at the top of a mountain, they had engineered a pecking order based on the time they reached their pitch, and they seemingly agreed to allow one tourist each. Every group of visitors hence acquired a symmetrical platoon of men and women clutching weather-beaten satchels, earnestly trying to sell the standard accoutrements – postcards, dog-eared guidebooks and Republican-era silver dollars with authentic dirt. Beggars were not so much banished by the Olympics as rebranded: a beggar with a packet of postcards is officially a beggar no longer, although he can be just as persistent.

'We are farmer,' they would say in broken English, pointing at the fields far below. 'This: tower,' pointing at the nearest battlement. In the logic of Chinese etiquette, this made them guides and you their grateful employer. They did not take kindly to being told that you did not need their assistance, as by the time they found this out they had already lost their place in the queue on the ridge and had to wait for their next turn.

But the hawkers of Simatai have themselves disappeared into history, swept away and repurposed as the city expands to meet the countryside. Simatai, once a dusty hamlet near a reservoir, has been reborn as a 'water town' – an olde-worlde evocation of Qing-dynasty life, with yuppie apartments scattered around the edges of picturesque lakes and charming canals. Artisans labour in boutique workshops in the shadow of the Great Wall. It all seems like a deliberate echo of the similar tourist traps that are dotted around the suburbs of distant Shanghai. Or, perhaps, for the more historically minded it recalls the quaint living theatre of traditional China that the Empress Dowager once arranged at the Summer Palace, where she could wander through an old-fashioned market and tell herself that nothing would ever change. Now the farmers of Simatai have a new performance: *pretending* to be traditional herders and weavers, putting on a show of sowing crops and gathering harvests to add a sense of traditional authenticity. They dress up as the people that they once were.

Although Beijing is now part of the twenty-first-century world, it still has its ghosts – or more accurately, immigrant ghosts from other parts of China. Folk tales and rumours no longer spread from tavern to tavern, co-opted into musical acts and storyteller routines. Instead, they leap across the internet and television. Beijing children terrify each other with tales of a haunted bus stop, where a disembodied voice calls out to the unwary, asking them the time. Damnation awaits anyone who is foolish enough to answer without turning around – it is the modern equivalent of the black-cloaked murderer of Beihai Park, but the story, like many modern Beijing residents, is not a native. Instead, it has entered local folklore from Hong Kong, where it first appeared.

Beijing is the Cinderella figure left in the shadows, never previously invited to the capitalist ball. Hong Kong is the brassy, loud, ugly sister, the one that got all the attention and all the money, suddenly swanning back home after a century of foreign suitors, dripping with glitz and glamour and high-tech trinkets. In the twenty-first century, Beijing is reinventing itself as a class act – the place with all the history and the monuments, the place where the emperors lived, the place where the government is, not forgetting the Eight Sights.

With Tiananmen still an international embarrassment, the Chinese government embarked on a series of initiatives designed to present a different side of Beijing – just as the Emperor of Perpetual Happiness had tried to fake historical continuity with his Eight Great Sights, the People's Republic pushed for the reinvention of many Beijing landmarks. Paramount among these was the grounds of the New Summer Palace, redefined as a site of historical pilgrimage, its renovation speeded up. The ruins of the Old Summer Palace, however, were left in their tumbledown state.

Today, they are a brief stroll from the high-tech district of Haidian. I wandered in bright sunshine among the wisterias and the willows, across little bridges with moon-shaped arches and along winding garden pathways. The ruins seemed carefully cultivated. Several of the lumps of fallen blocks, which I examined up close, turned out to be poured concrete – in China, even the ruins can be fakes. Meanwhile, there were lovely views across the mirror-still lake (which itself covered acres and acres) and the hills behind. I was sure, at moments, I could see the Great Wall snaking across the mountaintops in the distance, but I must have imagined it.

After an hour, I started to realise that it was all a bit samey. As I walked across another little moon-arch bridge, towards yet another willow-pattern copse of wisteria, I was to all intents and purposes completely lost. Yet another temple, yet another ruin, yet another bonsai bridge over a little pond. I'd already lapped myself and was walking around the same lake again, without realising.

Every now and then, an antique stolen in the sack of the Summer Palace comes on the international market. On the most recent occasions, China has bought back what was rightfully its own from a London auction house at a cost of millions of dollars. The Poly Group corporation has even inaugurated a museum on the eighth floor of its Beijing headquarters dedicated to artefacts stolen from China in ages past that have been repatriated with the company's outreach funds. A debate has raged for decades about the best manner to deal with the Old Summer Palace, with some officials arguing for the construction of a replica of its glory days, while others push for the original ruins as a far more evocative and moving sight. When one talks of tourists in Beijing, one is often talking of European tourists, and there is a strong and persuasive case for confronting such visitors with the ruins of their states' earlier military interventions.

Interesting Times

Real Communist-era treasures, such as the delicate propaganda posters that once hectored the faithful to Respect the Party and Destroy the Capitalists, are much harder to come by – their very fragility helping their value on the foreign market. But Beijing in the Olympic age would really rather prefer that foreign tourists stayed away from the socialist era. Sites and opportunities are certainly available to illustrate the achievements of Communism – particularly the Military Museum, occupying a forbidding Soviet-era power station and detailing the various injustices visited upon China by foreign powers. But the Communist era itself, with its headlines of grain harvests and tractor designs, is something of an off-colour joke, amusing in a dreary way for a while, until the poverty, persecution and purges of the Cultural Revolution stifle the smiles.

Upon seeing that I genuinely do have an interest in Mao-era propaganda, an antiques seller shyly proffers a small stack of crumbling posters – carefully aged, if not actually old. Her face goes as red as the East when I happen upon a slogan calling for the downfall of America.

'Times back then,' she says, 'were *interesting*.'

The great halls and staircases of the Forbidden City, the soaring towers of the Great Wall and the statuesque beauty of the Ming Tombs are much more likely to attract tourist dollars, at least from capitalist tourists. Once an embarrassment to town planners, the hutong alleys of Beijing are just as much a part of the modern city's heritage as the Forbidden City – perhaps more so, since a visit to them often pays directly into local pockets instead of government coffers. Pedicab drivers offer tourist trips around the few remaining hutongs in the city centre, where visitors can gawp at Qing-style buildings and the sight of people living on the edge of rural poverty, so close to the luxurious apartments of the Party faithful. But these, too, are dwindling, turning into re-enactments of what once was a genuine way of life and is now unaffordable to the people who work there. But this is not a uniquely Chinese experience – modernity exerts similar pressures on us all.

The Marco Polo Bridge is still where Marco Polo said it was, although much of what he said *about* it no longer holds true. It is not 'ten miles outside the city', since the metropolis of Beijing has sprawled across every scrap of available land in the place where once there was just an endless tract of marshland waving with reeds and thistles. Nor does the bridge serve its original purpose – not long after being given its new name by the Emperor of Hearty Prosperity, the 'Eternally Pacified' Yongding River took the hint and went away for good, leaving the bridge literally high and dry. Although floods and rains and the outflow from a 1950s reservoir may occasionally give it something to span, the bridge usually crosses little more than a shallow dip in the landscape, so overgrown that it looks more like parkland than anything else.

A few steps away from the ancient bridge, a sturdy concrete flyover takes care of modern traffic. This is the opening stretch of a highway that goes all the way to Macao, although the bridge's modern companion is less welcoming to pedestrians. You can still walk across the Marco Polo Bridge, but now it costs you US$2. There is still a trading post there, but it is a small and sorry open-air 'antiques' market selling bits of fake jade, Chairman Mao lighters that will surely be confiscated at the airport, feng shui compasses and doubtful fossils. Always, *always*, there are the Republican-era silver dollars – big round coins like Jubilee Crowns, bearing the fat, bald head of Yuan Shikai and smearings of dirt for that extra touch of authenticity. There were over 184 million minted, and all appear to be still in circulation, all boldly proclaiming that they are worth one dollar, all retailing for twenty and up.

The Great Wall remains the most powerful of symbols – its image is the first that any China visitor sees, snaking across every tourist visa. Entrepreneurs are redeveloping many more sections now, attempting to revitalise the economy of the mountains north of Beijing by making a visit there about more than just seeing the wall. Giant billboards out towards Simatai exhort tourists to come in the dead of winter, when they can ski in the Great Wall's shadow. The wall has also gained a modern, virtual analogue – the Great *Firewall* of China that blocks access from new forms of Western barbarity: our news, our erotica, our idle gossip. If you have Google as your internet homepage and a browsing habit that swings over to the BBC website several times a day, it can be a surprise to discover that those sites are simply not available to the internet user in Beijing.

The concept of heritage does finally hold some sway in Beijing. A Kentucky Fried Chicken franchise was ejected from Beihai Park after local pressure groups called it a capitalist step too far. Similar controversy surrounded the Starbucks branch in the Forbidden City, which gained a kitsch appeal among tourists before its unceremonious removal – the very silliness of it had a certain charm, akin to finding a Hello Kitty shop in Westminster Abbey. Despite my arch disapproval, I still felt compelled to use the ATM in the Forbidden City, just so I could say that I had. I took money from a hole in the wall at the Centre of the World, and I was charged US$5 for the privilege.

There are mixed feelings all round about the incursion of Western-style consumerism into the Forbidden City. After all, don't we *want* them to be more like us? We wanted them to buy mobile phones, didn't we? We wanted them to listen to the Beatles. We wanted them to sign trade agreements and consume along with the rest of us. As green politics rises to the fore, we also would like them not to make the same mistakes as us regarding pollution, demolition and emission, but perhaps it is already too late.

Tradition is a double-edged sword. Chinese tradition crippled women for a thousand years with foot binding; it castrated thousands of pauper boys to allow them to work in the palace; it tortured untold millions. The Forbidden City is no longer forbidden or forbidding – it welcomes visitors with their open wallets. Its brand identity, after all, is kept relatively muted, and it does good business – who are we to stop the Chinese from having a coffee at the Centre of the World, where eunuchs once tried to keep bicycles and eye-glasses away from the Last Emperor? The Western world already has its junk food and its corporate beverages, like it has the internal combustion engine and the nuclear power plant – should we begrudge the Chinese their coffees Venti and Grande, in the same way we begrudge them greenhouse gases?

But neither is modernisation a bed of roses. The rush of the modern is what hacked the Chinese coast up into treaty ports. Our desire to make the Chinese in our image is what force-fed them opium and smashed railway lines through ancient city walls. There are poor in London, too, in Washington, in Paris. Beijing was there before them all.

Chronology of Major Events

BC

c. 500,000	First arrival of Peking Man (*Homo erectus pekinensis*) in Zhoukoudian.
c. 400,000	Evidence of Upper Cave Man (*Homo sapiens*) at Zhoukoudian.
c. 25,000	Deer hunters camp on what is now Wangfujing.
c. 4500	Stone querns in the Beijing area used to grind acorns.
c. 2000	Bronze tool-working in the Beijing area.
c. 1200	Establishment of a walled city, Yanjing, Capital of the Swallows.
c. 1105	The Land of Swallows is a dukedom pledging fealty to the king of the Zhou dynasty in the south.
323	Duke Yi of Yan (the Land of Swallows) proclaims his own kingship, throwing off the authority of the Zhou kings. Beginning of the area's century as an independent state.
318	King Kuai of Yan abdicates, giving his throne to his chief minister, Zizhi.
315	Civil war and occupation by Qi (the Land of the Devout).
312	Withdrawal of Qi forces. Zizhi is deposed.

284	Yan army invades and occupies the Land of the Devout, led by Yue Yi.
283	Construction of a wall to mark the north of Yan's borders. This would later be incorporated within the first Great Wall.
232	Prince Dan returns to Yan without the king of Qin's permission.
231	Presumed commencement date of Prince Dan's assassination plot.
227	Jing Ke's assassination attempt on Ying Zheng, the King of Qin, masterminded by Prince Dan.
226	Qin forces storm the Land of Swallows in retaliation, forcing Prince Dan's father to flee north-east to Liaodong.
222	The last of the Yan defenders is defeated in Liaodong; official date of the fall of Yan. Surrender of King Xi.
221	Having conquered every rival state, the King of Qin proclaims himself the First Emperor of China.
215	The First Emperor visits the former Land of Swallows.
209	With the collapse of the Qin dynasty, the Land of Swallows is briefly independent once more.
202	The Land of Swallows is brought back within the empire, subsumed within the domain of the Han dynasty.

25   The former Land of Swallows is the power base for Liu Xiu, who subsequently becomes the first emperor of the Eastern Han dynasty.

250   Commencement of major water engineering projects in the area, designed to improve irrigation.

294   Local inhabitants, even foreign immigrants, pool their resources and labour to repair flood and earthquake damage in the region.

c.300   The city is renamed Youzhou, the Tranquil City.

314   The region falls under the influence of non-Chinese races, including the Xianbei and Toba – both regarded by the Chinese as 'barbarians'.

337–370   State of Former Yan

384–409   State of Later Yan

384–394   Western Yan

398–410   Southern Yan

409–435   Northern Yan

607   The region is linked with the South by a canal and brought back within the orbit of 'Chinese' rulers.

611   Youzhou is a staging post for armies of the new Sui dynasty for attacks on Korea.

644   The Taizong Emperor of the Tang dynasty returns to Youzhou in an attempt to complete his predecessors' military actions.

645   Taizong builds the Temple of the Origin of

the Law, a cenotaph in memory of Chinese soldiers fallen in Korea.

755   The city is a major base in the rebellion of An Lushan against the Tang dynasty.

759   A local attempts to proclaim a Yan 'dynasty', but fails.

917   Early incursions of Khitan tribesmen. The region is largely depopulated as Chinese colonists flee south for their own safety. Slow commencement of three centuries of North–South division.

1025   Only a couple of generations after their arrival, the Khitan rulers have been sufficiently sinicised to want to imitate the Chinese in the South. Examinations and sacrifices in Yanjing follow Chinese traditional models.

1115   The Jurchen tribesmen of the hinterland proclaim a new 'Chinese' dynasty, the Jin ('golden').

1120   The emperor of the Song dynasty unwisely attempts to oust the Khitans by arranging a deal with the Khitans' Jurchen rivals. Instead of restoring the region to the Song, the Jurchen take it for themselves. The city becomes Zhongdu, the 'Middle Capital' of the Jin.

1192   Completion of the Marco Polo Bridge.

1211   First Mongol attack on Zhongdu.

1215   Fall of Zhongdu to the Mongols.

1266   Khubilai Khan orders the reconstruction of

Zhongdu. Extensive remodelling of the water system. The city is renamed Dadu (or Taidu), the Great City.

1275   Arrival of Marco Polo in China. He writes of Dadu as 'Cambaluc', thought to be his transliteration of the Turkish 'Khanbalik' ('the khan's city').

1293   Completion of the new canal link to the South.

1345   Famines and floods lead to anti-Mongol unrest.

1368   Mongols driven out of China by the new Chinese Ming dynasty. The city is renamed Beiping, Northern Peace.

1371   Extensive reconstruction in Beiping, as the administrative centre of the emperor's fourth son.

1402   The fourth son of the late emperor seizes the throne, proclaiming himself to be Yongle, the Emperor of Perpetual Happiness. He relocates the capital to his own power base, and Beiping is named Beijing ('northern capital') for the first time.

1530   Construction of the altars to the Sun, Moon and Earth.

1601   Arrival of Matteo Ricci, a Jesuit missionary, in Beijing.

1644   Beijing is captured by the armies of the Manchus. The last Ming emperor hangs himself from a tree on Coal Hill, north of the Forbidden City.

1648   All Chinese residents are banished from the inner city of Beijing, which becomes a sector reserved exclusively for Manchus.

1694   The Russian community in Beijing begins to grow.

1745   Early work begins on the gardens of the Summer Palace.

1793   Visit by the first British ambassador to China, George Macartney.

1831   Flooding near the Marco Polo Bridge.

1896   Completion of the first railway between Beijing and Tianjin.

1900   The Boxer Rebellion and the subsequent occupation of the city by foreign troops.

1902   Cixi, the Empress Dowager, returns to Beijing by train.

1912   Abdication of the Last Emperor.

1916   Yuan Shikai fails in his bid to become the first emperor of a new dynasty and dies later the same year.

1919   Events at the Paris Peace Conference lead to the 4 May demonstrations in Beijing.

1920   First Chinese Communist organisation founded in Beijing.

1926   Police shoot and kill forty-seven anti-warlord protestors outside Tiananmen, the Gate of Heavenly Peace in central Beijing.

1928	Nanjing is the capital again. Beijing is named Beiping again.
1937	The Marco Polo Bridge incident sees the first shots fired in the Second Sino–Japanese War.
1938	The Japanese occupy Beiping and rename it Beijing.
1941	Japanese attack on Pearl Harbor. US and British residences in Beijing are occupied by the Japanese military.
1945	At the close of the Second World War, Beijing is contested between Chinese Nationalist and Communist forces.
1948	Communist forces surround Beijing.
1949	Surrender of Nationalists in Beijing. Chairman Mao proclaims the foundation of a new Communist state – the People's Republic of China.
1959	The tenth anniversary of the People's Republic of China sees central Beijing remodelled with Soviet-style architecture and a wide-open space in front of the Tiananmen gate.
1968	The army is deployed in Beijing in order to quell fighting between rival factions of Red Guards.
1971	Construction begins on the Beijing subway.
1972	Richard Nixon visits China.
1976	Death of Chairman Mao. His mausoleum is built in Tiananmen Square.
1982	In a change to Chinese law, all urban land is now the property of the state.

1985	Rioting in Beijing after the home team loses a soccer match against Hong Kong.
1986	Queen Elizabeth II visits China.
1989	Student demonstrations in Tiananmen Square are suppressed with tanks.
1990	Beijing hosts the Asian Games.
1992	Chinese legal reforms allow for the demolition of any building deemed 'dangerous' – this gives carte blanche for bulldozing huge areas of the city.
1993	Failed bid to hold the 2000 Olympics.
2001	Beijing's bid to host the 2008 Olympics is successful.
2003	SARS epidemic encourages outdoor drinking – close-packed Sanlitun bar culture begins to wane in favour of Houhai cafés.
2004	Oriental Plaza opens on Wangfujing, five times taller than previous city ordinances allowed.
2007	The Starbucks franchise is removed from the Forbidden City.
2008	Beijing Summer Olympics take place.
2011	Plans proposed for Jing-Jin-Ji, a megalopolis combining Beijing with Tianjin and much of the surrounding Hebei province.
2013	Beijing's pollution levels officially proclaimed 'hazardous to human health'.
2014	Power-station shutdown for the Asia-Pacific Economic Cooperation conference leads to a new slang term for skies improved by

	politically motivated beautification: 'APEC blue'.
2015	End of flat fees on the Beijing subway, reflecting the fact that some journeys on it should be far pricier. Now distance-based, the average journey price doubles overnight.
2019	Official opening of Beijing Daxing International Airport.
2020	China temporarily suspends tourist visas in the wake of the COVID-19 pandemic.
2022	Beijing Winter Olympics take place.

Further Reading and References

Opposite the Foreign Languages Bookstore, at the top of Wangfujing, there is a bronze statue of a gaunt Qing-era peasant pulling a rickshaw. The seat is empty, so that passers-by can be photographed in it, and the pulling poles have a gap in them to afford easy access. Not a minute goes by without someone clambering in for an opportunistic selfie, but there is much more to the statue than that.

The statue's name is *Xiangzi Pulling a Rickshaw*, and it commemorates Lao She (1899–1966). His best-known novel, published variously as *Rickshaw*, *Rickshaw Boy* or *Camel Xiangzi* is a satirical account of a wheeler-dealer in 1930s Beijing, who hopes to climb the social ladder by first renting and then buying a rickshaw. Xiangzi has very little luck – he is bitten by a donkey as a child, he is swindled by his customers and victimised by the authorities, and his toils come to nothing when his beloved rickshaw is stolen in an allegory of the false promise of capitalist dreams. That is only the beginning, as he moves into the potentially more lucrative world of camel droving and beyond. But Xiangzi is not merely a satirical character; he is a passionate Beijinger, deeply reluctant to leave the city that has raised him – 'filthy, beautiful, decadent, bustling, chaotic, lovable' Beijing. His fate was rewritten in the Communist era, when Lao She was persuaded to tack on an ending more suitable for the Communist utopia of 1949.

Lao She himself was not so lucky, hounded to his death during the persecutions of the Cultural Revolution. His body was found floating in Taiping Lake, but even that is no longer there – it was filled in some years ago, and now it is just another street, up near the Second Ring Road, close to an orthodontic hospital and a subway drivers' dormitory.

General Accounts

There are several excellent books about Beijing and its history, including Stephen Haw's *Beijing: A Concise History* (Routledge, 2007) and M. A. Aldrich's *The Search for a Vanishing Beijing: A Guide to China's Capital Throughout the Ages* (Hong Kong University Press, 2006). Aldrich is rich in anecdote and trivia, and displays a flâneur's eye for Beijing life. He is also the author of an unexpectedly detailed history of Beijing told entirely from the point of view of its Muslim population. Featuring photographs by Lukas Nikol, his *The Perfumed Palace: Islam's Journey from Mecca to Peking* (Garnet, 2010) is a captivating exercise in telling a familiar story through an unfamiliar framework.

For a real sense of the gritty, slippery reality of chronicling the city's many rises and falls, Jasper Becker's *City of Heavenly Tranquillity: Beijing in the History of China* (Penguin, 2008) is highly recommended, not least for its scathing account of how the old city has been destroyed since 1997.

In the early years of the twenty-first century, Mao Xiang was a guide offering walking tours to foreign tourists. Although he has now relocated to Canada, his legacy lives on in *Beijing Walks: Like a Flying Feather Through the*

Hutongs (Foreign Languages Press, 2012), a 471-page compilation of sixteen historical tours of the city. Reprinting his notes to what appears to be an exacting degree – second-person asides, restaurant tips and all – this idiosyncratic book contains a wealth of historical information, providing unexpected depth and insight. Born and bred in the hutongs, Mao plainly mourns the loss of many landmarks, although his book was published at a fortunate time when the destruction of the old city was finally curtailed, and hence remains up-to-date – if there is one book worth buying *in* Beijing, this is it.

For an insider's-eye view, Liu Aifu's *English Tour Guiding in Beijing* (China Tourism Publishing, 2014) is an absorbing English-language textbook for would-be guides, giving them all the details they are likely to need while shepherding foreigners around. As one might expect, certain modern topics are conspicuous by their absence, but it's particularly good on the big sites like the Forbidden City and the Temple of Heaven. It also has an unexpectedly intriguing troubleshooting chapter on such matters as what to do if one of your clients dies mid-trip.

Somewhat haphazardly translated, such that one often needs to speak Mandarin to actually understand it, Liu Baoquan's *Beijing Hutong* (China Travel & Tourism Press, 2008) is a toponymic study of Beijing, concentrating on the evolution (or, as he would have it, the 'evolvement') of its various place names. There is much fun to be had here in the historic euphemisms shunted onto places once known as Donkey Meat Alley or simply Doghole – the mind boggles. Look here for glimpses of Beijing's past, trivia about the name-origins of many streets and stations, and the complex historiography of the word 'hutong' itself. For the true completist, the book also includes a nine-page list of Chinese celebrities – everybody from the Last Emperor to Li Hongzhang – and their one-time hutong addresses.

Xu Chengbei's *Old Beijing: In the Shadow of Imperial Throne* (Foreign Languages Press, 2001) is often frustratingly apocryphal or uncritical but contains valuable slice-of-life sections, pictures and anecdotes not repeated elsewhere.

Publishers and Authors

Hard to find outside China, but readily snapped up at the Foreign Languages Bookstore in Wangfujing, are a number of bilingual guide books by the Beijing Art Photography Press (now part of the Beijing Publishing Group, somewhat counter-intuitively abbreviated as BPH), useful both for the researcher and souvenir hunter. Titles from the likes of the Foreign Languages Press are also a bargain in China, whereas they are often sold abroad at a hefty markup.

It is difficult to choose representative Chinese authors from among the many thousands who have written about Beijing. The aforementioned Lao She is one of the city's most famous sons, and Howard Goldblatt's *Rickshaw Boy* (Harper Perennial, 2010), the most recent of many translations of *Camel Xiangzi*, remains mordant and insightful. Its account of the young men who 'mortgage their youth' in pursuit of nebulous success, with the odds weighed against them, still speaks to the daily lives of the taxi drivers, shopgirls and, yes, even rickshaw men, who still ply their trade in Beijing.

Any investigation of modern books about Beijing must wade gingerly through entire shelves of self-indulgent, lazy romans-à-clef by hateful twenty-somethings, in which charmless ciphers only look up from their smartphones to complain about their lattes. This, too, is a faithful glimpse of contemporary Beijing life, albeit no fun to read. However, a few modern novels have inherited some element of Lao She's soul, such as Yan Geling's *The Banquet Bug* (Hyperion, 2007), published in the UK as *The Uninvited* (Faber, 2007), in which a ne'er-do-well discovers he can eat like a prince at public functions as long as he poses as a journalist. Similarly, Xu Zechen's *Running Through Beijing* (Two Lines, 2014) lionises an unlikely hero in the form of an ex-convict hustling pirate DVDs.

Ma Jian's *Beijing Coma* (Chatto & Windus, 2008) tells the story of the post-Tiananmen generation through the experience of a man shot in the head during the protests, who is left musing about his life while China transforms around his comatose form. A similar approach, framing the last thirty years as collective amnesia about what really matters, can be found in Chan Koonchung's *The Fat Years* (Doubleday, 2011).

The Land of Swallows

For the story of Pierre Teilhard de Chardin, his China expedition and his star-crossed love for Lucile Swan, see Amir Aczel's *The Jesuit and the Skull: Teilhard de Chardin, Evolution and the Search for Peking Man* (Riverhead Books, 2007). Gao Xing's *Peking Man Site at Zhoukoudian* (BPH, 2004) offers a good introduction to the archaeology of the site. Statistics in this chapter were taken from Gina Barnes's *The Rise of Civilization in East Asia: The Archaeology of China, Korea and Japan* (Thames & Hudson, 1999). My quotes in this chapter from the *Intrigues of the Warring States* are taken from J. I. Crump's *Chan-Kuo T'se* (University of Michigan, 1996).

North and South

The translations from the *Ballad of Mulan* in this chapter are my own from the original Chinese, but you can read it in English in its entirety in Arthur Waley's *Chinese Poems* (new ed. Routledge, 2012). The story of the woman with several husbands is taken from *Women in Early Imperial China* (Rowman & Littlefield, 2002) by Brett Hinsch. For the story of Nezha, see E. T. C. Werner's *Dictionary of Chinese Mythology* (Julian Press, 1961). Discussions of the architecture of the city and its uses in warding or encouraging spirits, rely upon Jeffrey Meyer's *The Dragons of Tiananmen: Beijing as a Sacred City* (University of South Carolina Press, 1991). For many customs and rituals from old Beijing, including the stories associated with the bridge of magpies, see Derk Bodde's *Annual Customs and Festivals in Peking as recorded in the Yen-ching Sui-shih-chi* (Henri Vetch, 1936). The story of 'Ruby' is from *Beijing Legends* by Jin Shoushen (Foreign Languages Press, 2005) – a compilation of folk tales from throughout history, favouring the Ming and Qing periods; it also forms an important source for my next three chapters.

Khanbalikh

Timothy Brook's *The Troubled Empire: China in the Yuan and Ming Dynasties* (Harvard, 2010) offers a general introduction to the period, provocatively and entertainingly framed in terms of reports of 'dragons', which he cross-references with droughts and floods symptomatic of the Little Ice Age. For an account of the Grand Canal that makes special reference to the labours of Guo Shoujing, *China's Imperial Way* (Odyssey, 1997) by Kevin Bishop and Annabel Roberts traces the whole thing all the way from Hong Kong.

My quotes from Marco Polo's *Travels* use the out-of-copyright Henry Yule translation, but the reader with a genuine interest in a readable and critically edited version would do well to use Ronald Latham's (Penguin, 1958). For an assessment of Polo in historical context, Stephen Haw's *Marco Polo's China: A Venetian in the realm of Khubilai Khan* (Routledge, 2006) is an excellent study. My own books *Marco Polo* (Haus Publishing, 2007) and *A Brief History of Khubilai Khan* (Robinson, 2010) also offer histories of the Mongol period in Beijing.

The Forbidden City

For an in-depth treatment of the alleged relationship of Beijing to the transmogrified corpse of Nezha, the best source is Arlington and Lewisohn's *In Search of Old Peking* (see above). Qi Luo's bilingual *The Great Wall* (BPH, 2004) has some lovely stories about the Ming dynasty's most enduring relic. Zhang Heshan's *Whispers from the Wall: Great Wall Folktales Told Across the Centuries* (China

Intercontinental Press, 2009) is also in both Chinese and English and, as the title implies, is an unapologetically uncritical collection of any stories the author has heard about the subject.

For the Eight Great Sights, see Aldrich's *Vanishing Beijing* (Hong Kong University Press, 2006). Hu Hansheng's *The Ming Tombs* (BPH, 2004) is a fine guide to the Ming necropolis, although its travel recommendations are understandably out of date – Hu cannot possibly have imagined that within little more than a decade the site would be within reach of the Beijing subway.

For the Forbidden City, there are numerous books available – I have referred specifically to Leng Pu's *The Palace Museum* (BPH, 2004). As for the backstabbing and double-crossing of the emperor's harem, you can't do much better than Shang Xizhi's entertainingly tawdry *Tales of Empresses and Imperial Consorts in China* (Hai Feng, 1994).

For the complex and dramatic tale of Wu Sangui and his supposed treason, my own book *Coxinga and the Fall of the Ming Dynasty* (History Press, 2005) has it all in spades, as well as the prolonged aftermath, in which the last of the Ming loyalists held out for another forty years.

Victor Meignan's *From Paris to Pekin Over Siberian Snows* (Swan Sonneschein and Co., 1885) is my source of quotes from the cantankerous French traveller. Paul Reinsch's *An American Diplomat in China* (Doubleday, Page and Co., 1922) is also quoted.

'Peking'

George Macartney's *An Embassy to China* (Longmans, 1962) has been republished in a lavish Folio Society edition (2004).

Everybody and his dog wrote tell-all accounts of the larks they had in the Legation Quarter, particularly after the derring-do of the Boxer Rebellion. Diana Preston's *A Brief History of the Boxer Rebellion: China's War on Foreigners, 1900* (Robinson, 2002) is the standard modern work on the Rebellion itself and collates many primary sources. Readers who want to read actual correspondence can try the centenary edition of *The Siege of the Peking Embassy, 1900* (The Stationery Office, 2000). The future US president Herbert Hoover and his wife were also among the besieged legations – a story glossed in just a handful of pages in most biographies but dealt with at greater length in Gary Nash's *The Life of Herbert Hoover: The Engineer 1874–1914* (Norton, 1983). Putnam Weale, a pseudonym for Bertram Lenox Simpson, published his own account of the siege and of the city in which it took place, as *Indiscreet Letters from Peking* (G. Bell, 1906). Notably, foreign accounts are usually big on the siege and conspicuously more reticent about what Weale calls the 'sack' afterwards, when the Eight Powers Army looted the whole town.

The reader interested in the early twentieth century is advised to start with Julia Boyd's *A Dance with the Dragon: The Vanished World of Peking's Foreign Colony* (I. B. Tauris, 2012), which offers glimpses of many primary sources and will facilitate some considerable cherry-picking. Quotes in this book from Alec Tweedie, cattily entertaining and often presciently accurate, are from her *An Adventurous Journey: Russia–Siberia–China* (Thornton Butterworth, 1926), which compared Beijing with the newly Bolshevik Moscow.

Some other quotes from this period are sourced from Ellen LaMotte's *Peking Dust* (Century, 1919), a book with great insights into the expat community of the time and some apt commentary on the way the Chinese were being exploited by the European powers. LaMotte is particularly good on the opium trade and on the forgotten 'twelve demands' issued by the British in 1917 with regard to Tibet.

Despite devoting much of its page count to life in the Summer Palace rather than the place promised in its title, 'Princess' Der Ling's *Two Years in the Forbidden City* (Moffat, Yard and Co., 1911) is notable for its intimate and sympathetic portrait of the Empress Dowager as a capricious and deluded but ultimately good-hearted old lady. It is loaded with some wonderful quotes from its subject, including 'Do you know, I have often thought that I am the most clever woman that ever lived,' and 'What is dancing?'

The most famous foreign resident of the period was arguably the man chronicled in Hugh Trevor-Roper's *Hermit of Peking: The Hidden Life of Sir Edmund Backhouse* (Penguin Books, 1978; earlier editions lack useful revisions). Backhouse lives again, in all his scandalous glory, in *Décadence Mandchoue: The China Memoirs of Sir Edmund Trelawny Backhouse* (Earnshaw Books, 2011), Derek Sandhaus's painstakingly reconstructed edition of his sordid fantasies of life in the brothels of the old city. Australian readers may prefer Cyril Pearl's *Morrison of Peking* (Penguin Australia,

1970), which chronicles the life of the man who briefly lent his name to the street now known as Wangfujing.

For a real insider's-eye view, of course, there's always 'Henry' Puyi's *From Emperor to Citizen: The Autobiography of Aisin-Gioro Pu Yi* (Foreign Languages Press, 1989), a Party-approved memoir by the Last Emperor, or at least by his ghostwriter Li Wenda (there are rumours that novelist Lao She also helped buff it up). Reginald Johnston's *Twilight in the Forbidden City* (4th rev. ed., Soul Care, 2008) is less liable to have been redacted by the Party.

Northern Peace

Arlington and Lewisohn's *In Search of Old Peking* (1935; my references are to the 1967 edition from Paragon Book Reprint Corp.) deserves to be filed among the greatest of the general accounts above, but is listed here because it was written in the closing days of Northern Peace and strongly reflects the city of that era. Written at roughly the same time and imparting even greater detail for the reader of Chinese is Ma Zhixiang's 1935 *Beiping Lüxing Zhinan* ('A guide to Beiping for travellers') – the version I have referred to is the annotated modern edition, *Lao Beijing Lüxing Zhinan* (Yanshan, 1997). For an English-language account of the city's development in the Republican era, and what vestiges of that time remain today, Madeleine Yue Dong's *Republican Beijing: The City and its Histories* (University of California Press, 2013) is a good place to start.

Paul French's *Midnight in Peking* (Viking, 2011) is an enthralling account of the last days of the old city, pertinently characterised by the gruesome murder of an unfortunate Russian refugee girl near the Fox Tower. Meanwhile, as the subtitle suggests, John Blofeld's *City of Lingering Splendour: A Frank Account of Old Peking's Exotic Pleasures* (Hutchinson, 1961) is an uncensored account of his time as a young man in the city during the mid-1930s, crowded with drug addicts and fallen women, with the ominous clouds of war gathering in the north-east.

Empty Spaces

There are several lively accounts of life in the Communist era, including Patrick Wright's *Passport to Peking: A Very British Mission to Mao's China* (Oxford University Press, 2010). Delia Jenner's *Letters from Peking* (Oxford University Press, 1967) presents an interesting snapshot of a young scholar's life in the Cultural Revolution period. Frances Wood's *Hand Grenade Practice in Beijing: My Part in the Cultural Revolution* (John Murray, 2000) is not quite the Spike Milligan romp promised by the title, but still engages amiably with the absurdities of its day. Perhaps the most unexpected chronicle of late Mao-era Beijing can be found in *The China Diary of George H. W. Bush* (Princeton, 2008), compiled by Jeffrey Engel from the notes and tapes of the man who was America's de facto China ambassador from 1974–5, before diplomatic relations officially thawed and the author went on to bigger things.

The best book on recent urban change is Michael Meyer's *The Last Days of Old Beijing: Life in the Vanishing Backstreets of a City Transformed* (Walker & Co., 2009), an account of hutong life by an American resident who provides copious details on the city's history while also documenting the advance of the bulldozers as the Olympics loomed. Harriet Evans chronicles the same period and place in *Beijing from Below* (Duke University Press, 2020), with an epilogue updating the story a decade later. For a glimpse of the infighting and deals behind the scenes to make Beijing what it is today, see Wang Jun's *Beijing Record: A Physical and Political History of Planning Modern Beijing* (World Scientific, 2011).

Beijing Welcomes You

Anne-Marie Broudehoux's *The Making and Selling of Post-Mao Beijing* (Routledge, 2004) is particularly good on the politics of the Olympic bid and the changes wrought upon the city as a result.

Rachel DeWoskin's *Foreign Babes in Beijing: Behind the Scenes of a New China* (Granta, 2005) is a snapshot of twenty-first-century life by a PR consultant who inadvertently became a Chinese soap opera star. Pallavi Aiyar's *Smoke and Mirrors: An Experience of China* (Fourth Estate, 2008) is a lively account of Beijing in the early twenty-first century from a refreshingly non-European angle.

A more considered look at changes in modern Beijing, and perhaps changes to come, can be found in Stephanie Tansey's *Recovery of the Heart: Dialogues with People Working Towards a Sustainable Beijing* (New World Press, 2012). At times, it feels like the author has rounded up all her friends in a pub and called it research; even so, there are many provocative and thought-provoking ideas here for a greener Beijing and of the problems Beijing is liable to face in the interim.

Quirky and entertaining, *Hiking in Beijing* (Foreign

Languages Press, 2010) is an update of a 2003 guide by a collective largely comprising foreign ramblers. Six years is a long time in the Beijing countryside, and some of its locations are liable to have been turned into yuppie enclaves by now, but it still offers an interesting account of country life in the shadow of the Great Wall.

Great Prosperity

Coverage of Daxing's construction largely derives from Ian Johnson's 25 November 2018 article in the *New York Times*, 'A mammoth new airport shows China's strengths (and weaknesses)'. For details of the huge Jing-Jin-Ji project, see Mark Preen's article 'The Beijing–Tianjin–Hebei integration plan' in *China Briefing*, 26 April 2018.

In the thirteen years that have passed since the publication of this book's first incarnation, many wonderful books have brought new perspectives. Jonathan Chatwin's *Long Peace Street* (Manchester University Press, 2019) is an idea I wish I had thought of – a snapshot of Beijing as revealed through the author's marathon walk along the 28-mile length of Chang'an Avenue, from one end to the other. For an account of the way that Beijing has continued to redact and refashion its own history, Louisa Lim's *The People's Republic of Amnesia: Tiananmen Revisited* (Oxford University Press, 2014) is an eye-opening read.

The paperback edition of this book drops the hardback's time-sensitive gazetteers of Beijing tourist sites and restaurants, but if you are interested in the story of China's cuisine, I recommend my own *The Emperor's Feast: A History of China in Twelve Meals* (Hodder, 2020).